Sempre Avanti!
The Responsibility of Privilege

by

Richard L. Hirsch
with Peter Weisz

©MMXX • All Rights Reserved

Richard L. Hirsch

Copyright© 2020 by Richard L. Hirsch
All rights reserved. No part of this publication may be translated, reproduced, stored in a retrieval system or transmitted, in any form or by any means, electronic, mechanical, photocopying, recording or otherwise, without express written permission from the author.

Published by **E&R Books**, an imprint of:

Peter Weisz Publishing, LLC
7143 Winding Bay Lane
West Palm Beach, FL 33412   USA
peter@peterweisz.com

Hirsch, Richard L. July, 2020
    Sempre Avanti! / Richard L. Hirsch with Peter Weisz
    Memoir—Biography—Business —Judaism—Self-Help—Religion—Personal Improvement

ISBN: 9781716704178

Printed in the United States of America by Lulu Press, Inc., www.lulu.com
1 2 3 4 5 6 7 8 9 10

Dedication

to Larry

Richard L. Hirsch

The Responsibility of Privilege

Not only his favorite catch-phrase, "Sempre Avanti" or Always Forward, is a definitive description of one man's personal philosophy that has propelled him into key leadership positions in both the worlds of commerce and philanthropy.

In this revealing and amusing retrospective, Richard Hirsch shares the high and low points of his exemplary and exceptional life's journey. Emerging from a Jewish immigrant family that founded the nation's largest manufacturer of kitchen stoves, Richard was immersed in the principles of "*Tzedakah*" and "*Tikun Olam*." You will read how he learned, at an early age, about the true "Responsibility of Privilege."

Becoming the youngest C.E.O. of a Fortune 500 company at age 29, Richard soon realized that the firm was floundering. Through struggle and stamina, he fielded a team that eventually succeeded in not only turning the company's fortunes around, but building it into a powerhouse force in the commercial kitchen equipment industry.

In this passionate memoir, you will discover how Richard not only continued his family's legacy of philanthropic support for crucial causes, but how, through tenacity and determination, he advanced those causes to new heights of achievement.

Business captain. Philanthropist. Family man. Richard Hirsch's life journey can well serve as a blueprint for the aspiring young business leader and social activist. In this book, he not only provides us with an engaging backward look, but also shares his vision for the future as he urges us all to always keep moving forward. Sempre Avanti!

ACKNOWLEDGEMENTS

I would like to extend my special thanks to the following individuals without whose generous assistance this book could not have been written:

- Jonny Friedman, my nephew.
- Rochelle Hirsch, my sister-in-law.
- Larry Gross, my lifelong friend and colleague.
- Daniel, Michelle, and Adam; my children.
- Peter Weisz, my collaborator.

  and, most of all, for her untiring editorial work, endless research, and unflagging moral support,

- Elaine Bedell, my wife.

Richard L. Hirsch

Table of Contents

Introduction 9

Chapter One, Losing Larry 11

Chapter Two, Little Me 17

Chapter Three, The College Kid 25

Chapter Four, The Price of Privilege 35

Chapter Five, My Father's House of Worship 47

Photo Album, Pt. I 55

Chapter Six, The Making of a Manager 73

Chapter Seven; The Full Monte 79

Chapter Eight, The Welbilt Story, Pt. I 87

Chapter Nine, The Welbilt Story, Pt. II 97

Chapter Ten; People, Product, Finance 103

Photo Album Pt. II 109

Chapter Eleven, Family Matters 127

Chapter Twelve, With A Little Help From My Friends 143

Chapter Thirteen, Tikkun Olam 153

Chapter Fourteen, Thinking Ahead 169

Family Tree 175

Richard L. Hirsch

INTRODUCTION

When my friend, Lee, asked for a favor it was useless to say no. With the perfect trifecta of looks, charm and wit, he was going to get his way, one way or the other, so of course I said yes when he asked if I could help his friend find an apartment to rent. It made no difference that I was busier than ever, never leaving my office before 9 PM after spending a full day in the market, or that I didn't really handle rentals, just sales. Lee said his friend needed help and that he wasn't going to let some barracuda broker take advantage of him. I asked him to tell me about his friend, and all he would share was: "He's a good man. Take care of him."

So that's how, two days later, I found myself waiting to meet Richard Hirsch in the lobby of the now defunct Mayfair Hotel on Manhattan's Park Avenue and 65th Street, where one of the only two apartments that met his needs happened to be located. I was standing near the elevators when I felt a tap on my shoulder. I was totally unprepared for the megawatt smile and robin's egg blue eyes that greeted me. He reached out to shake my hand—that quaint pre-Corona virus gesture of respect—and I noticed his elegant, well-groomed hands and how comfortable my hand felt in his. No doubt about it, he had me at "Hello."

The book you are about to read was something Richard had talked about doing since I had first met him, but you know the saying about the best laid plans of mice and men. Then, somehow, right before the pandemic gripped the world and stopped it on a dime, all the pieces fell into place. An abyss of unfilled time opened, a writer with the same vision appeared just as Richard's desire to tell his story all converged, and, Voila!: The Book.

It is my hope that those who read this memoir and who do not know Richard well will get a sense of who he is and that those who do know Richard will learn much more about him. I further hope that younger family members, who only think of Richard as that nice old guy who picks up the bills, will get an eye-opening peek at the young Richard, full of energy and passion, hard working and disciplined, funny and smart, and completely devoted to his family, his friends, his business, and his people. The good news is that he still is all of those things.

I couldn't have foreseen 30 years ago, and wouldn't have believed it if I could have, that we would end up happily married. I'm also happy to still be taking care of him, happy that he fit me into his world, and happy that Lee was right in his terse assessment of "He's a good man." A *really* good man.

—Elaine
July, 2020

Richard L. Hirsch

Chapter One
Losing Larry

Our son, Lawrence Hirsch, of blessed memory.

"There is no tragedy in life like the death of a child. Things never get back to the way they were."
— Dwight D. Eisenhower on the death of his 3-year-old son, Ike, Jr.

At the time that I was about the same age as his stricken son, General Dwight D. Eisenhower, the Supreme Commander of Allied Forces in World War II Europe, was employing these very words to console parents of US soldiers killed on the beaches of Normandy after the D-Day invasion. Back in 1920, Eisenhower's own first-born son had suddenly fallen ill and succumbed to Scarlet Fever; a disease he had contracted from a servant. As stated, things never got back to the way that they were.

Years later, neither Joyce, my wife at the time, nor I could have anticipated that we would someday be able to attest to the tragic truth in Ike's words.

During the summer of 1972, the presidential election that would see incumbent Richard Nixon crush Democrat George McGovern was in full swing. That August, the Washington Post carried a brief page-five article about a mysterious break-in at a place called The Watergate. As was often the case in those days, I was on the road fulfilling my duties as the youngest CEO of a US publicly-traded corporation: Welbilt, a maker of domestic and commercial kitchen appliances. Before I had left home this time, I was concerned about our five-year old son, Larry. He was running a temperature of 101 and exhibiting flu-like symptoms. After I arrived at my destination, Joyce called and told me she was planning to take Larry to the ER at South Nassau County Community Hospital.

When we spoke again on the following evening, I detected a tremor in Joyce's voice as she explained: "They looked him over at the hospital and they think it might be mono. They gave him some oral antibiotics. His temperature is at 100 and he says his head hurts." This sounded serious, but not life-threatening.

Since his birth in 1967, Larry had endured a spotty medical history. He was plagued by a variety of conditions including asthma. While his younger brother, Daniel, age 3 at the time, remained at home, Larry attended the Malibu Beach Day Camp, located off of Lido Road on the opposite end of Long Beach. Our home was situated in the scenic village of Atlantic Beach, about an hour's drive from my Maspeth office in Queens. Atlantic Beach had received some notoriety during those times thanks to the GODFATHER novel and movie. Atlantic Beach was the fictional home of Sonny Corleone, the Godfather's oldest son.

"I'll be home tomorrow afternoon," I told Joyce. "Give him a big kiss from me."

When I landed back at LaGuardia the following day, I was met at the airport by my sister Carole and her husband, Mickey. I was unprepared for the shock they were about to deliver. Carole and

Mickey had accepted the sad duty of informing me that our son had died.

I learned that before his death, Larry's symptoms had worsened. His lips had started turning blue, he was vomiting blood, his temperature was up to 106 and he had begun experiencing mild seizures. Tragically, Larry died mysteriously after being in the hospital for less than 24 hours.

It took several months and an autopsy to discover the cause of Larry's death. I arranged to have all of his medical and autopsy records transferred from the hospital to a team of top diagnosticians at Brown University, my alma mater. After conducting an exhaustive scrutiny of the data, the doctors at Brown made the following determination: Larry's death was due to overwhelming and diffuse encephalitis. This is caused by an arthropod-borne (mosquito) virus called LACV (LaCrosse Encephalitis Virus). Once infected from a mosquito bite, the patient is most likely to come down with Eastern Equine Encephalitis (EEE). This is a neuro-invasive disease caused by an acute viral infection. Older children are typically able to fight it off with antibiotics, but in Larry's case, given his medical history, he simply did not have sufficient strength or resistance to combat the infection.

We surmised that Larry must have been bitten by an infected mosquito while he was attending summer day camp. In those days, each summer would see newspapers filled with headlines like: "Worst Encephalitis Epidemic in Decades Flares as States Vainly Battle Mosquitoes." In the year alone that Larry died, there were five reported cases of equine encephalitis. As is often the case with grieving parents, I sought someone to blame for this intense tragedy. I considered filing a malpractice complaint against the physician who treated Larry, but my attorney advised that we would have a difficult time making a case and so we dropped it.

Joyce and I tried to go on with our lives, but like General Eisenhower had observed, things never really got back to the way they were.

While the ensuing grief process was guided by our family's Jewish heritage (we observed the ritual seven days of *Shiva* and the thirty days of *Shloshim*), I recall that it was a particularly heart-wrenching time for my father, Henry Hirsch, to whom Larry was something more than merely a grandson. He was an emblem of our family's future in America; the beneficiary of all that our family had worked to achieve. It was, after all, for Larry and his grandchildren's future that my father had built the Fifth Avenue Synagogue. Both he and my mother were beyond devastation.

It did not help matters that we were living in the Dark Ages of grief counseling. It would be five years before the very first book on the subject, THE BEREAVED PARENT by Harriet Schiff, would be published. The book was a masterpiece of inaccuracy. Schiff was not a mental health professional. She was a mother who had lost a ten-year old son and by way of therapy, had published a poorly-researched volume that generated numerous myths and misconceptions. Foremost among these was the contention that 90% of all bereaved couples experience divorce. This oft-quoted, but entirely inaccurate statistic, soon snowballed and became the common wisdom of the day. Subsequent research has categorically shown, however, that losing a child has no significant impact on the likelihood of divorce.

Perhaps it was due to this widely held misconception serving as a self-fulfilling prophecy that both Joyce and I were resigned to the inevitability that our marriage could not survive this crisis. And despite the fact that we stayed together and had two more children over the next two decades, Michelle and Adam, the dark cloud that was the loss of Larry, never fully lifted.

The impact on Joyce was profound. Although she had always been reserved in conversation, she was incredibly well-read and highly knowledgeable on a wide range of topics. After Larry's death, she became increasingly withdrawn, perhaps unwittingly erecting walls to protect herself from the inescapable pain of losing a child she so adored. In our impenetrable fog of grief, I must admit that I was of little help to Joyce. I was contending with my own pain while trying to console my stricken and aging parents. Looking back, I am only able to imagine the torment that Joyce went through daily. She had been a doting loving mother to both Larry and his younger brother, Daniel. This was her entire life. While I at least had my work to serve as a temporary distraction, Joyce, as was customary in those days, was a stay-at-home mom. She was surrounded by constant reminders of Larry's life at every turn. I was pre-occupied with building our company, going on business trips, and working late hours—even when I was in town. To Joyce's enduring credit, she did not become bitter or resentful of me. She was, and remains to this day, a wonderful mother and role model for all of our children.

Somehow we made it through those difficult years, largely due to her strength and moral integrity. Once we were certain that our children were all on a solid footing, we found that we were unable to reconcile many of our marital issues and sadly decided to end our marriage in the early 1990's. Although many of our friends presumed that Larry's death had been somehow responsible for our divorce, I do not honestly believe that this was the case.

Losing Larry did, however, become an inflection point in my own life. It provided me with a new-found appreciation for the importance of family. I was blessed to have the unwavering support of my staff at Welbilt, including a true stalwart: my Brown University frat brother, Lawrence Gross. Larry was an indispensable ally over the many years we worked together at Welbilt. He stepped up to the plate and assumed my responsibilities during my period of grief and mourning. Thanks to him, I was able to use this downtime to conduct a complete inventory of my goals, my values, and the ultimate direction of my life. It triggered my transformation from a fully focused, full-time business leader to a man who today is able to look back with fondness and pride at all three major spheres of my life: The professional, the personal, and the philanthropic.

This book contains glimpses from my life's journey—brief stories and snapshots that are intended to explore some of my life's high points as well as some of the low points. I invite you to join me on this journey to gain a glimpse of who I am and what I believe. Whether you are a member of my family, a former business associate, a community service colleague or a member of the public, I believe that you will find something of interest and something of value among these pages.

And you will also come to understand why I have dedicated this book to Larry's memory. His passing did, in fact, insure that "things never got back to the way they were." You will see that while certain things were changed for the worse, so many things in my life were ultimately changed for the better. Thank you for sharing these defining moments and memories with me.

Chapter Two
Little Me

Seated on the steps of the Seiden Hotel in Palm Beach, Florida.

"The hardest thing in life is knowing which bridges to cross and which bridges to burn."

— Bertrand Russell

It did not take my family long to figure out which bridge to cross out of Brooklyn—the place I was born during America's last summer of innocence before the attack at Pearl Harbor plunged the our nation into World War II. Two weeks after my birth in May of 1941, my parents, Henry and Myrtle Hirsch, headed across the Marine Parkway Bridge to put down roots in the lush lawns of Old Lawrence, Long Island. Moving to Lawrence, a bedroom community near Hempstead, and one of the storied "Five Towns" that include Cedarhurst and the Hewletts, represented a step up the social ladder for our family. It was a declaration of sorts that the Hirsches, a first-generation Austro-Hungarian immigrant family, had "made it" in the *Goldeneh Medina* of America. Although some Jewish families did so, I'm pleased to report that we did not burn any bridges to our heritage.

My grandparents, Louis and Esther Hirsch, were known by the name Hirschlag, which indicated that our ancestors had originally hailed from the agricultural *shtetl* (village) of the same name in southwest Poland. Tiny Hirschlag exists today and, at last count, consists of 23 households, none of them Jewish.

Louis and Esther departed Poland in 1886, emigrating from their home in Debica (*Dembitz* in Yiddish) outside of Krakow in the Kingdom of Galicia. The first Jews arrived to Debica in 1675 and (according to the community's official history) quickly began exerting a positive effect on the town's economy. As a result of the First Partition of Poland in 1772, Debica became part of the Kingdom of Galicia when it was annexed by the Hapsburg Empire. As the Enlightenment spread throughout Eastern Europe during the 19th century, the Jews of Galicia enjoyed both the blessings and the curses of their newly-endowed citizenship. In addition to being taxed, my grandfather found that he was at risk of being conscripted into the Emperor's army where he would be forced to serve for 25 years or until his death—whichever came fist. Joining the massive first wave of Eastern European Jewish immigration, he and my grandmother decided to flee and, as depicted in the final scene of Fiddler on the Roof, set sail for America.

Having shortened their last name to Hirsch (perhaps in honor of the famed German Orthodox rabbi, Samson Raphael Hirsch, who had died the previous year, but just as likely due to an immigration clerk at Ellis Island wishing to save the trouble of writing a lengthy unfamiliar name), my grandparents settled in the New York community of East Williamsburg where they produced nine children—all boys. My father, Henry, born in 1903 was the second youngest (see Family Tree chart on page 176).

Henry received an upbringing that spanned World War I and prepared him well to face the Great Depression as a member of America's Greatest Generation. He absorbed business *sechel* (wisdom) from his older brothers and an intense immersion in Jewish tradition and culture from their parents. In 1937, Henry married the woman who would become my mother. The former Myrtle Getelson, was the possessor of "movie star" good looks—she resembled a young Lauren Bacall—coupled with a vivacious and cosmopolitan charm. My sister, Carole was born soon after in 1938 and I came along in 1941, followed two years later by the birth of my younger brother, David.

My earliest memory arises from an incident some five years later, after our family again relocated from Lawrence; this time to a twelve-story Fifth Avenue high-rise on the Upper East Side of Manhattan. My parents quickly enrolled me into kindergarten at the Ramaz School, a private Modern Orthodox Jewish day school located on East 85th Street. As it did then, the school includes grades pre-school through 12, offering secular classes taught in English and Judaic studies in Hebrew. I may only have been five years old, but I was already demonstrating signs of being headstrong and determined. And I determined very quickly that Ramaz Kindergarten was not a place that I liked whatsoever.

On the third day of classes, my mother escorted me to school and was standing in the front foyer speaking with my teacher when I decided that I had had enough of the place. I turned on my heel and scampered out the door out onto the bustling street. Looking down, my mother caught a glimpse of the closing front door and both she and my teacher gave chase. I was easily able to out-pace them and would still be running had I not been halted in my tracks by a red stoplight at the corner of 85th Street and Park Avenue. I had been trained to only cross the street on the green, so while I waited dutifully for the light to change, my mother caught up, took me firmly by the hand and brought me back to the school.

The teacher suggested that I may have been suffering from "departure anxiety," caused by a fear that "Mommy was not coming back for me." She suggested that for a while my mother stay with me during the day. Mom agreed and would sit in the school lounge for a few hours while I was in the kindergarten classroom nearby.

After a few weeks, this was no longer necessary and she was able to drop me off and leave immediately without fear that I might run away again.

I remained at Ramaz up through the fifth grade. It was at this level that I ran into a problem with my secular teacher. I was ten years old and had become even more headstrong over the years. A few weeks after the start of the semester, I announced to my parents: "You've got to take me out of Ramaz. I really hate my teacher this year." This led to some animated and agitated discussions between my parents.

"I've heard that Columbia Grammar School is excellent, Henry," my mother offered.

"What about his Jewish education?" countered my dad. "He's got to start studying for his Bar Mitzvah soon. He can't do that at CGS."

"We can do that privately," she said. "and I know just who to ask."

As my stalwart ally, a role she would often fulfill over the years to come, my mother had all the answers and, fortunately for me, in this dispute she prevailed and I was transferred to CGS. Known today as Columbia Grammar and Preparatory School, CGS is the oldest nonsectarian private school in the country. Located in a brownstone off of Central Park West at 5 W. 93rd Street, it was founded in 1764 by Columbia University. That connection ended after the Civil War when the school became fully autonomous—although Columbia instructors would often teach at the school. CGS became co-ed during my Freshman year when it merged with the Leonard School for Girls. I loved my new school and became an outstanding student, although I have remained friends with many of my old classmates from Ramaz to this day.

The question of my Jewish education was soon addressed when my parents hired the services of the sexton from the Jewish Center to provide me with private tutoring. Despite its name, the Jewish Center was, and remains one of America's premier modern Orthodox synagogues. It was founded in 1918 by well-to-do Jews who were moving into Manhattan's Upper West Side. Located in a neoclassical building on West 86th Street, the synagogue served not only as a spiritual home for the community, but also provided a venue for cultural, social and recreational activities. It was affectionately known in those days as "the *shul* with a pool." The synagogue's first rabbi was Mordecai Kaplan, the founder of the Jewish denomination known as Reconstructionism. Its pulpit was also graced by such luminaries of the Jewish world as Dr. Leo Jung, founder of Agudath Israel and Torah Umesorah, as well as Dr. Norman Lamm, future Chancellor of Yeshiva University.

My tutor, the Reverend Henry Julius, would visit several times a week shortly after I arrived home from school in the afternoon. After making sure I was wearing my *kipa* (skullcap), he would always light up a huge cigar before embarking on our studies—stinking up our entire apartment. To this day whenever I smell pungent cigar smoke, it invariably invokes the memory of those late afternoon lessons.

Eventually we turned to my bar mitzvah preparation. These days kids are typically asked to read excerpts from their assigned *Sidra* (a weekly portion from the Torah that is read during *Shabbos* services), but back then we were expected to read the entire *Parsha* (same as *Sidra*) aloud in Hebrew directly from the Torah scroll. Because my thirteenth birthday fell between two *Shabboses* I was offered a choice between the two *Sidras*. Not surprisingly, I chose the shorter one called *Behar* which comes from Chapter 25 of the Book of Leviticus. Interestingly, *Behar* lays out some of the ancient Israelite laws of a practical nature that would evolve into part of today's commercial code. It deals with property rights, the transfer of land, expounds on the Sabbatical seventh year and forbids any acts of fraud and usury.

My bar mitzvah took place in 1954 at Congregation Zichron Ephraim (today known as the Park East Synagogue) on Manhattan's Upper East Side. The synagogue was established in the late 19th century as an Orthodox bastion against encroaching Reform Judaism that was making inroads in the area's affluent Jewish community. The building is known for its moorish revival architecture and its remarkable pair of asymmetrical twin towers on either side of a prominent Rose Window. My bar mitzvah ceremony was officiated by Rabbi Zev Zahavy, a dynamic speaker whose sermons appeared regularly in the pages of the New York Times. The synagogue has been home to numerous celebrated congregants over the years including Edwin Schlossberg, husband of Caroline Kennedy.

On that Saturday morning my mother, noticing my understandable nervousness, offered me one of her phenobarbital tranquilizers. It did the trick. I sailed through the service without a glitch or a flutter. As I said. She was my eternal ally.

Unlike many of the other bar mitvahs at the time (as well as these days), there was no lavish blow-out celebration on Saturday night. My father, a believer in humility and modesty, had arranged for a meaningful and dignified reception that afternoon in the synagogue. He had imported a special Jewish choir whose spiritual singing everyone enjoyed. My father did not wish to put on a big show in front of the several area rabbis whom he had invited to our *simcha* (joyous event). I believe I learned more from his example of humility than from the Torah teachings I had been studying for my Bar Mitzvah.

As I mentioned, our high school merged with a girl's school during my Freshman year. It was then that I began thinking more about my image and how I appeared to my fellow classmates, both male and female. I began to realize that I was among the more privileged members of the student body that contained kids from various socio-economic backgrounds. My father had arranged for me to be delivered to and picked up from school in his private limo. I convinced the chauffeur to drop me off and pick me up several blocks away from the entrance to conceal this fact. Even at that early age, I was sensitive to being pointed to as "that rich kid" and simply did not wish to be perceived as bragging or showing off our family's wealth. Despite my efforts at trying to be viewed as just a "regular guy," the nickname I was branded with by my classmates was "Bucks," as in money.

With no more than fifty kids in each grade, I grew to develop lifelong friendships with many of them. Eighteen graduates of CGS's Class of '59 gathered for our 60th reunion in 2019. I was recognized at that event, not only for having received a Good Citizenship Award at graduation, but also for earning the rank Salutatorian (academically second highest) of our graduating class. That meant that I was required to deliver a Salutatory Address during our commencement exercises held in Carnegie Hall. I recall that I had some help with that speech from a very special CGS teacher, Mr. George Gordon, who still lives fondly in my memory.

Mr. Gordon sort of adopted me when I was in Middle School and I stayed under his wing till my graduation from high school. He was more than a mentor. He became a true friend and was simply an all-around terrific guy. I admired him for not only the strength of his thinking, which was substantial, but also for his quirky sense of humor. I still recall the day he arrived to Biology class carrying two dozen eggs.

"Today," he announced, "I am going to show you that you are not as strong as you think you are. I need three volunteers to come forward."

After demonstrating that the eggs were raw by cracking one into a glass bowl, Mr. Gordon then placed an egg into the palm of the first student's right hand. He folded the student's fingers over the egg. Next, he placed another raw egg between the forefinger and thumb of the next volunteer; one finger pressed against each end of the egg. Finally, he simply handed a raw egg to the the third student with the words: "Here. Hold this in your hand and put your hand over the bowl."

Mr. Gordon then instructed the first student to squeeze the egg. He did so, but the egg did not break. He next told the second student to squeeze. Again, the egg remained intact. Finally, he told the third student to squeeze and the egg cracked, getting raw egg all over the student's hand before it was caught in the glass bowl.

Mr. Gordon explained that a hen's egg is a marvel of nature. Strong, yet fragile at the same time. "How else," he inquired, "could an egg support the weight of a big fat mother hen sitting on it without breaking? Yet, when a little baby chick wants to come out, he is able to crack the shell with just a few pecks of his tiny egg tooth." Gordon went on to explain mathematically how the shape of the egg allows for it to resist being damaged when pressure is applied evenly, as in the case of the first two volunteers, yet breaks easily whenever uneven pressure is applied.

This lesson was one that has stayed with me and one that I have relied upon over the years in my negotiations with suppliers, competitors, labor unions and others. If I am being pressured in one direction, I try to find another source of pressure in the opposite direction. In this way, I am less likely to crack.

Although I did not become aware of it until many years later, at the same time that I was welcomed to a life of comfort and privilege in America, Jews in Europe were undergoing a lethal pressure of the worst kind. I recall, as an adult, looking at a list of Holocaust victim's names at Yad Vashem in Jerusalem. I spotted one, Juta Hirsch, who was born the same year as I was in 1941 in a town called Skole in the former Kingdom of Galicia. Was she a relative? Who knows? Juta was murdered at age two, along with her parents, in a concentration camp outside of Lvov. She was killed for only one reason. She was born a Jew. But for the grace of God and the fortitude of my grandfather, that poor child could have been me. As I write these words today, I understand more fully than ever before, that the blessed life I was born into comes with an obligation. A moral imperative to not only remember, but also to actively assure that such things do not happen to our people ever again. This, then, is the true "Price of Privilege."

Chapter Three

The College Kid

Paddles from both my fraternities.

"Educating the mind without educating the heart is no education at all."

— Aristotle

I am not sure if I was an early bloomer or a late bloomer, but I know for a fact that I bloomed at CGS. After my Bar Mitzvah, a time when some young teenagers start to slack off, I went the other way, studying Latin and French and earning top grades.

Being one of the tallest kids in the class, I played a lot of basketball and I loved the game. But, as it would do often during my formative years, my Jewish observance created complications. Most of the games were on Friday night, *Shabbos*. While a rabbi might find it objectionable, my parents did allow me to play basketball on Friday afternoons after school. But I was not permitted to violate the sanction against riding in a car from sunset on Friday through sunset on Saturday. This prohibition is based on the fact that igniting a fire on *Shabbos* is strictly forbidden and by driving a car, you are causing the spark plugs in the engine to create combustion.

While I was able to ride public transportation or be transported by car to various venues to play in the Friday afternoon basketball games, I was unable to ride home since it would be dark by the time the game was over. Hence, I was forced to walk home from each basketball game—often between twenty and thirty blocks—to join my family for *Shabbos* dinner.

I was taught to be *"Shomer Shabbos."* The term means "Watchman of the Sabbath" and it refers to Jews who observe Halakhic law strictly in terms of the *Shabbos, Kashruth* (dietary laws) and all the *mitzvot* (commandments). This meant sacrifice. I was unable, for example, to attend my high school graduation party since it was held on a Friday night. While CGS was mostly populated with Jewish kids, only a handful, like me, were *Shomer Shabbos*.

Once I realized that my basketball skills on the court were not good enough to earn me an athletic scholarship, I began to lose interest in the game. By my Senior year I was no longer a member of the varsity team and like most high school Seniors, I was, by that point, concentrating on getting into college. I also faced an obstacle on this front. That obstacle was my dad. He wanted me to stay in New York at all costs and, in deference to his wishes, I applied to Columbia. But at the same time, I also applied to Yale, Brown and U. Penn (the University of Pennsylvania) in addition to my anchor schools, Franklin and Marshall. I didn't really demonstrate a great interest in the latter two, so, not surprisingly, they rejected me.

I vividly recall sitting for my interview on a Thursday in the Columbia Admissions office. The following Monday I received a phone call that I had been accepted! Not only was I contacted by Columbia, but, in a highly unusual move, they contacted the principal at CGS and said: "Richard Hirsch. We want him." Although I have no direct evidence, it appears in hindsight, that my overnight acceptance by Columbia had been pre-arranged by someone pulling the strings behind the scenes. Someone, such as Henry Hirsch, who wanted his son to remain in New York and had the clout to see that it got done.

My mother, always my advocate, did not share my dad's desire to keep me close to home. Plus she was good friends with a professor at Brown. I was accepted there and decided to attend since its location, in Providence, Rhode Island, was only a two-hour train ride away. This was important because it meant I was able to often travel home for the weekend. During those times, my father was adamant about me being in synagogue on Saturday morning. As the synagogue's founder, he had a seat of honor near the Eastern wall close to the altar. He would often twist around to make sure that his college kid son had made it to services on time.

My most salient memories of my Freshman year at Brown are painful ones. I was in a bad situation that resulted in a good deal of misery and depression. I had been assigned to a room with two other freshmen who may have been Jewish, but, if so, they were so highly assimilated and non-observant that one could not easily tell. This made meal times problematic. Brown, of course, is not a Kosher school. So this meant I could not consume most of the menu items offered on the student meal plan. This also meant I had to obtain food from alternate sources and not break bread with my classmates. This alienation was heightened by the fact that I was in the habit of donning my *t'fillin* (phylacteries) and praying every morning. I wound up being forced to *daven Shachrit* (recite the morning prayers) every day hidden away in a staircase or an isolated corner of the hallway. The whole situation was awkward and uncomfortable.

Due to my religious observance, I refrained from taking courses that offered classes on Saturday and this fact resulted in non-stop academic issues. For example, several of the classes I did take scheduled final exams on Saturday. In consideration of my observance, I was permitted to arrange for each exam to be administered on Saturday night after sunset. I would be placed into a room all by myself where I would remain until I completed the test.

By comparison, keeping kosher in this environment was a much bigger challenge. But little by little by little, and through the help of others, I met the challenges and managed to remain at Brown for four years without starving to death. One source of assistance was the local chapter of the Jewish student association known as Hillel. Hillel had an off-campus house with a small cooking area, but it was not a kosher kitchen. Fortunately, my father's company, Welbilt, was in the commercial kitchen equipment business, so he quickly arranged to have new stoves, ovens and refrigerators installed at the Hillel House. My mother located a Kosher chef who was hired to come to the Hillel kitchen once a week to prepare my week's evening meals and store them in the refrigerator. This was before microwaves became popular, so I ate most of my suppers cold. Of course, the Hillel meal was only one meal per day. For breakfast and lunch I had to fend for myself, selecting my food very carefully in the communal dining hall.

Shabbos was another story. I'm not sure how they made the connection, but somehow my parents contacted a well-known Jewish lawyer in Providence named Archie Smith. Smith also had a child enrolled at Brown and the family all kept Kosher. The Smiths lived two blocks from the Brown campus and they would invite me to join them for Friday night *Shabbos* dinner as well as lunch the following day. They essentially adopted me as their *Shabbos* son and for the four years I attended Brown, I could invariably be found at the Smith house on those weekends that I did not go home to New York. The Smiths became my surrogate religious parents and I will never forget the debt I owe them for their kindness and for making it possible for me graduate from an Ivy League college as an Orthodox Jew.

As mentioned, I was unable to take all the classes I wished because of the Saturday restriction and so, academically, I was just getting by. On top of that, I wasn't around the campus that much. I would travel home for every Jewish holiday, secular holiday, and many weekends. This resulted in my earning poor grades during my Freshman year. Towards the end of the year, it was time for the traditional fraternity rushing rituals. I had made some friends and they encouraged me to try to get in to one of the better frat houses, Pi Lambda Phi. The problem was that the house was very exclusive and typically only accepted a handful of boys as pledges. With my lackluster grades and lack of social or athletic involvement, getting into Pi Lambda Phi was next to impossible. Guess what. I got in. I suspect they checked out our family's net worth and determined that accepting me might result in a sizable pay off down the road. They weren't wrong.

Pi Lambda Phi, or PiLam, as it was known, was founded at Yale at the end of the 19th century. It opened a chapter house at Brown in 1929 that remained open through 1963. During my Junior year, my frat brothers and I became unhappy with the national PiLam organization and decided to disaffiliate. While not a Jewish fraternity, per se, there was a large contingent of Jewish students both back then as well as today. Some of the more illustrious PiLams over the years included sportscaster Howard Cosell, filmmaker Stanley Kramer, composer Richard Rogers, Senator Arlen Specter, Baseball Hall of Famer Sandy Koufax, businessman Mark Cuban, and Baseball Commissioner Bud Selig. We eventually re-affiliated with another national fraternity, Alpha Pi Lamda. Hence, today I am the proud owner of not one, but two engraved fraternity paddles.

I moved into the PiLam house at the beginning of my Sophomore year knowing only one other pledge. I had previously selected him as my roommate during my Freshman year. As it turned out, my-roommate-to-be did not return to Brown in the fall, so I was left unattached. There was only one other pledge who likewise had lost his roommate resulting in the two of us "accidentally" bunking together. This was my *"shiddach"* with the person who would eventually become one of my closest friends and my most trusted business colleague, Larry Gross. Ironically, at the end of my Sophomore year, when everyone was afforded the opportunity to switch and pair up with a new roommate, the only two fraternity members who opted to remain together were Larry and me.

It did not take long to discover that Larry was not only incredibly intelligent, he was a person of great integrity. He and I formed a bond that was strengthened as we both became highly involved in the affairs of the fraternity, both serving as officers. Larry was elected president of the Faunce House Board of Governors, Brown's student union, and an officer of the student government. He was very helpful to me when I was setting up the kosher kitchen at Hillel, as I'll explain a bit later. Larry and I found that we worked well together on projects and programs and often spoke about joining forces in the business world later on. Meeting Larry Gross was undoubtedly one of the most positive outcomes of my attending Brown University.

Larry's father was a journalist and a member of the Washington press corps. He was also a Navy man and had encouraged Larry to apply for a Naval ROTC scholarship, which resulted in the Navy paying for Larry's college education. Upon graduation, Larry received a commission in the regular Navy and served for two years aboard the famed naval destroyer, the USS The Sullivans. He spent the remaining two years of his service working in communications security at the Office of the Chief of Naval Operations in Washington DC, during which time he was able to attend Georgetown University law school. It was during those years that Larry developed and honed his considerable organizational and management skills.

I had stayed in communication with Larry during his Navy stint and when he was discharged in 1967 I presented him with an offer. At that point I was pretty much running the show at Welbilt and I explained to him that the company was in dire straits financially. I told him I needed a capable team to help me turn things around, and asked if he would consider moving to New York to join me. To my good fortune, he agreed.

Larry's first assignment was in Human Resources where he gained an overview of our company's operations which at that time consisted of a one million square foot metal-bending factory in Queens with a workforce of 1100 employees. He deftly handled our collective bargaining negotiations with the Teamsters and the various other labor unions we were required to deal with. These skills would become vital in later years as together we negotiated mergers and acquisition deals that would result in our company's rapid growth.

The following year, after I had assumed the CEO title, I realized that if I was going to be successful without burning myself out, I would need someone capable and trustworthy to serve as my right-hand man and occasional surrogate. I immediately decided on Larry and asked him to assume the title of Assistant to the President. Happily for me, he again agreed. Larry and I would go on to successfully run Welbilt together for many years and I am proud to say that his ability and friendship were key to our many achievements and our ultimate success.

Living in the frat house did not make the challenge of keeping Kosher any easier. Once again, my father came to the rescue. He wanted to make sure that I was able to stick with the dietary laws and not be tempted to give them up at college. Henry had a close relationship with Cantor Bernard "Barney" Bloomstein at the Fifth Avenue Synagogue. Cantor Barney, who worked for free at the synagogue, was the owner of Bernan Foods, a manufacturer and purveyor of Kosher canned foods such as stuffed cabbage. My father had arranged for Barney to send me regular care packages in the mail filled with Kosher food items that I could store in my room. This at times proved humorously problematic. I remember being called to the house telephone.

"Is this Richard Hirsch," said the distraught voice. I said that it was.

"This is Mr. Carlyle at the post office and we received a package addressed to you," he stated hurriedly.

"Do you want me to come down and pick it up?" I asked.

"No, you can't do that," he replied.

"Why not?"

"Because it exploded," he exclaimed. "We've got this damned gunk all over the post office (referring to the stuffed cabbage) and it stinks to high heaven. We'll get it cleaned up, but tell whoever sent that to you not to send stuff like that in the mail anymore."

I agreed to do so, but I knew they would keep on sending it anyway.

In addition to the care packages from Barney, I would also bring back boxes of food after each visit home. My parents had a live-in cook who would prepare meals for me that I would wrap up and bring back to my frat house room. The problem is that in the beginning I had no access to a refrigerator and I was afraid the food might spoil if it wasn't kept cool. So, since it was winter, I decided to place some of the food outdoors on my window sill, hidden out of sight under some tree branches. But I would not always remember to bring the food back in.

I recall getting a call from the school groundskeeping office in the spring. Someone had complained about some debris stuck to the outside of my window at the PiLam house. Evidently I had forgotten some packaged food items outside and the birds had eaten it, leaving behind the wrappers which had become frozen to the famous ivy vines that covered the brick walls of our building. I managed to clean up the mess and swore to get my hands on a proper refrigerator.

Over time I began to build up a support structure that I would rely upon to make it possible for me to matriculate as an observant Jew at Brown. Among the most supportive was one of the school's pastors, Charles Baldwin. Pastor Baldwin had a great deal of respect for my adherence to Jewish law and he sort of took me under his wing during my years at Brown. He was extremely helpful when I needed to arrange for time off to observe Jewish holidays, for example. He had an inside track with the school administration and could get just about anything done.

Many years later, in the 1990's, Hillel wanted to recognize me for my support and proceeded to dedicate a kitchen in my honor. I decided to express my gratitude to Charles Baldwin by placing his name on the dedication plaque. He had retired from Brown by this point, but he somehow heard about my gesture and sent me a beautiful note of gratitude.

Not everyone was cooperative, however. The head of the Hillel program was not all that crazy about the new Kosher kitchen equipment we had installed. But in the end we convinced him we had done the right thing. Whereas we started out with only three students: a Brown guy, a Bryant College student and me, eventually they were attracting dozens of kids to the best Kosher kitchen in town. Although the Kosher kitchen has expanded over the years and is still active today, it did so despite, not because of, the support of the Hillel administration.

My years at Brown were devoted to obtaining a classical liberal arts education. My major was Philosophy which was also filmmaker Woody Allen's major. at CCNY.

"I got kicked out of college," Woody once quipped, "because during a Philosophy exam I was caught looking into the soul of the student sitting next to me."

Because of my screwed up schedule, twisted to accommodate my *Shabbos* observance, it was necessary for me to attend summer school at Harvard to make up some classes, such as chemistry, that I needed for my degree.

What I found at a Harvard was a very different sort of chemistry. I'm referring to the type of chemical reaction that occurs when man meets woman and heat is generated. More about this in the next chapter.

Richard L. Hirsch

Chapter Four
The Price of Privilege

Plaque memorializing the terrorist attack at the Dolphinarium on June 13, 2002.

"The more privilege you have, the more opportunity you have. The more opportunity you have, the more responsibility you have."

— Noam Chomsky

Due to an erratic schedule caused by my commitment to religious observance, I found myself needing to catch up academically after my Freshman year at Brown. I had the good fortune, if only for a short time, to attend Harvard to try and make up some needed credits. I learned that if I signed up for Chemistry during summer school at Harvard, and passed the class, I would not need to take Chemistry at Brown. I wasn't very fond of Chemistry or Biology, so this solution appealed to me.

As luck would have it—bad luck, that is—I was placed into a class filled with Harvard pre-med students who all simply sparkled at Chemistry. I was struggling along, lost in a sea of bunsen burners, test tubes and over-achievers. I managed to finish the course, but was in so far over my head that I decided to throw in the towel and skip the final exam. Astonishingly, Brown decided to accept the credits from Harvard based on the fact that I had survived the entire tough, pre-med chemistry course. I'm happy to report that good luck also prevailed during my Harvard summer, as it was there that I met the future Mrs. Hirsch. Like me, Joyce Finker was taking a summer class at Harvard to supplement her studies at Syracuse.

One day I noticed a very striking girl sitting on the steps of the Harvard Library talking with a friend. Although I walked around them several times and was clearly noticed, I was ignored by both. Fortunately, a short time later I attended a mixer and both of the girls were there as well. Joyce was tall, very attractive, and had a certain presence that made her stand out in a crowd in an elegant way. I struck up a conversation with her and learned that Joyce's friend was a girl named Fran, who was seeing a fellow named Benji Brown, a good friend of mine from New York. It wasn't long before we were all double-dating. In those days, our family would spend summers in Atlantic Beach and Joyce's family lived in the scenic Five Towns community of Hewlett Park nearby. This allowed us to connect repeatedly over the summer breaks. During school semesters, we maintained the relationship on a long-distance basis, cemented by Joyce's beautifully hand-written letters.

Joyce was a true academic achiever and managed to obtain her bachelor's degree in just three and a half years. As my own graduation approached, I naturally began giving some thought to my future. I had a good-looking girlfriend and an Ivy League education. What more could any guy ask for in life?

My father and I were not in the habit of having heart-to-heart discussions, so I was a bit surprised when one *Shabbos* after services, he informed me that he wanted to have a talk. He got right to the point.

"So, Richard. What are you going to do now?"

"Well, Dad," I replied, "I'd like to take some time off and travel. You know, see the world." This was a few years before the Vietnam-era military draft got rolling, so I was not at risk of seeing the world from the inside of a Humvee in Danang. "You don't need to do that," he said, sweeping the idea aside dismissively with his hand. "Come to work at Welbilt. Full-time."

I had worked at the commercial kitchen equipment company my father had founded during a portion of my Junior year and I found that I liked it. The work was interesting and there was little pressure.

"That sounds fine, Dad," I said. "But I'd really like to take some time off before settling into the job. You understand." He pondered this a minute as if this statement somehow "did not compute" with his ingrained work ethic. Finally, he said:

"Okay. Take two weeks off and then report to the plant." And that was that. End of chat.

The Welbilt Stove Company was founded in 1929 in Maspeth Queens, New York by my father, Henry Hirsch and his brother, Alexander, known by everyone as A.P.. The company achieved stunning growth through expansion and acquisition so that by this point, in 1963, it was producing equipment under such brand names as Frymaster, Delfield, Merrychef, and Merco. In 1955 Welbilt had acquired the nearly 100-year old stove-maker, Garland, making Welbilt the oldest player in the industry. A few years later, Frymaster landed its first food chain account with Kentucky Fried Chicken and has been making the Colonel's deep-frying equipment ever since.

When I arrived through the doors of its main facility, I was directed to the shipping department in the basement. It appears that my dad had recently seen the Broadway show "How to Succeed in Business Without Really Trying" which recounts the meteoric rise of an ambitious corporate climber all the way to the top spot as CEO. Hence I was to begin my orientation at the bottom of the totem pole in the shipping department. I again found the work enjoyable and interesting and after five months I was moved to another department. All part of my on-the-job orientation.

As I moved from department to department, I got an intimate glimpse of the inner workings of a large and complex industrial operation. Predating the show "Secret Boss," I did not reveal my identity to my co-workers for fear that knowing I was the boss's son would prompt them to treat me differently. Despite my wish for anonymity, my co-workers would sometimes figure out my true identity and then the fawning behavior would begin.

I was living at home with my parents during this period and spending all my free time with Joyce. But pretty soon, the Selective Service began rearing its ugly head. Not long after assuming the presidency in 1963, after the JFK assassination, Lyndon Johnson began his escalation of US troop levels in Vietnam. This required ramped up manpower and hence the draft was re-instated to fill the void. I soon felt the hot breath of the US Army breathing down my neck.

At that time, the Selective Service offered deferments for a variety of circumstances. I had graduated out of my undergrad student deferment, so one of my only options was to secure a marital deferment. Uncle Sam was only drafting young single men at that time. If you had a spouse, you were safe...for now. Joyce and I had spoken about getting married in a few years, but with this development we decided to move things up a bit and have the wedding sooner rather than later. Uncle Sam was my best man.

There was no formal "down on one knee" proposal. Everyone had assumed for years that we would be married, so it was sort of a given. Among these was Joyce's father who, sadly, passed away shortly before our wedding and was unable to walk his daughter down the aisle. Nevertheless, the wedding was a joyful affair despite the circumstances, held on the Ides of March, 1964 at the renowned Plaza Hotel in Manhattan. Of course, in consideration of the fact that my bride was still observing the traditional year of mourning the death of her father, there was no orchestra or music of any sort.

Our first home was on Yellowstone Boulevard in Forest Hills, just over the Queensborough Bridge, near the Welbilt facility in

Maspeth where I worked. And a mere twenty minutes from my parents' home.

I was definitely learning the ropes at Welbilt, but I was learning something more. I was now privy to seeing how my father spent his days. These, were the years of prime involvement with Fifth Avenue Synagogue. So, I was not surprised to see him come in at around 11 am, after having spent four hours at the synagogue helping to run the place efficiently and effectively. Occasionally, I would stop by his office and observe how a good portion of his time was spent devoted to Jewish causes. As his reputation as a philanthropist grew, more and more solicitors would come through the door. Among these were the steady stream of Jewish *shnorrers* (fund-raising solicitors). These were the bearded, black-hat rabbis who came seeking a handout on behalf of their impoverished yeshivas back in Israel.

Perhaps my father's most favored charitable cause, before founding the Fifth Avenue Synagogue, was a school in the Kensington area of Brooklyn called Yeshiva Torah Vodaath. Billing itself as "the mother of the Yeshiva movement in America," YTV has been providing Torah-true education for more than a century. At the time my father became involved, the school was situated in a single building and had an enrollment of 150 students. Today, it occupies three hi-rises in Flatbush, while operating satellite programs in Monsey, Marine Park and Boro Park, and enjoys an enrollment of more than one thousand pre-school, elementary, and high school students, as well as rabbinic candidates.

My father became involved with Yeshiva Torah Vodaath through his friendship with two celebrated figures from that era: the well-known accountant, Louis Septimus, and a financial wizard who served as the regional director of the IRS in the 1920's, Harry Herskowitz. Herskowitz literally dedicated his life to the vision of building a Torah community in the United States and convinced many, such as my father, to join him in this crusade. Today the school is housed in the Harry Herskowitz School campus. It contains a dormitory that was underwritten by my father and dedicated to the memory of my grandfather, Louis Hirsch.

Another influencer who attracted my father to Yeshiva Torah Vodaath was the esteemed Lithuanian Rabbi Yaakov Kamenetzky who served as the school's *Roish* (principal) from 1945 to 1968. Reb Yaakov (as he was affectionately called) led American Jewry in issues of *halachic* (legal) and spiritual guidance until his death in 1986, when he was bestowed with the title of *"Chakima D'Yehudai"* (the wise man of the Jews). Today, Rabbi Kamenetzky's grandson, Rabbi Mordechai Kamenetzky serves as the *Roish* of the presitigious South Shore Yeshiva and Mesivta Toras Chaim in Hewlett, New York.

My mother was also deeply involved with Yeshiva Torah Vodaath. She had established a foundation in her mother's name, The Rose Getelson Sunshine Fund, whose purpose was to operate the school's summer programs as well as other projects. She, along with two of her friends, would put together the summer programming each year. Bear in mind that neither of my parents attended this school, nor did any of their children. Yet, they became one of its primary benefactors.

My father's reputation for philanthropy preceded this period and even preceded my birth. He was so well known as a Jew of means and a willingness to help, that a nonstop flow of letters arrived to his door daily during World War II. Each letter contained a plea for his help to rescue a child, a family, or a community from the clutches of the Nazis. I recall him showing me one such envelope that contained a desperate plea from Europe. The sender did not know his address so he addressed the letter only to Henry Hirsch, USA. And it reached him.

My father had established a charitable foundation that he would employ to distribute gifts to those causes he supported. His greatest joy was sending out checks to people who contacted him for his help. He worked with many of the rescue organizations and those offering sustenance to Jewish refugees in displaced persons camps in Europe. While he never spoke about it, I suspect that he was involved in some clandestine operations below the radar, during and after the war, that sought to get Jews out of Europe and into Palestine.

During those years, my mother was a very effective fund-raiser on behalf of Jewish rescue causes. With her stunning good looks and sublime fashion sense, women would attend her functions just to see what she was wearing. Unlike my father, she was committed to more than the religious side of Judaism. She was more of an all-purpose Jew. Her support for Jewish causes often tended to lean towards the secular and domestic. She was very active in what was then known as the United Jewish Appeal (UJA) that raised money for Jewish social service programs in American communities. One of her pet causes was Project Renewal which, despite her non-Zionist leanings, she found meaningful. The program was jointly created in 1977 through the Israeli Government and the Jewish Agency under the leadership of Prime Minister Menachem Begin. Project Renewal had connected prosperous American Jewish communities with 140 disadvantaged ones in Israel. Donations collected would go directly from the US community to the Israeli one to which it had been linked. This project has since been dissolved.

Foremost in her work on behalf of Project Renewal was my mother's dedication to the community of Miftan Alon, outside of Tel Aviv. My mother was recruited as a Miftan Alon advocate by legendary Tel Aviv mayor, Shalom "Cheech" Lahat. Our family had issued a grant to Miftan Alon High School, an institution that caters to distressed students, ages 14 to 18, who have left, been expelled or have given up on the formal education system—some of them having emerged from prison. Through its educational, therapeutic, and rehabilitation programs, the school serves as a safety net and fosters students' vocational skills at a Function Center called The Lion & The Turkey. We were able to supply their training kitchens with high-quality institutional kitchen equipment. In addition to providing underprivileged kids with job training in such areas as event planning and banquet cooking skills—skills they need in order to join the workforce—vocational training also empowers students by cultivating a sense of confidence, responsibility, decision-making and other life skills. An after-school program called Pure Expressions also teaches students how to create beautiful Judaica items and jewelry.

The school features a full-service beauty salon used to train future stylists and beauticians. The facility was donated, at my mother's suggestion, by industrialist Ron Perelman, who at the time, was a member of the Fifth Avenue Synagogue and a true friend of the family. Ron's support was very much appreciated.

In addition to vocational training and offering psychological therapies, the school also engages in preparing at-risk teenagers for military service. Without the benefit of such training, most of these kids would not be acceptable by the Israeli military (IDF). The school is sending dozens of students per year to the military and most are able to get their lives pointed in the right direction while in uniform. This innovative program proved so successful that it has been adopted all across Israel.

Miftan Alon was regarded as one of the crowning achievements of the Project Renewal program thanks to the efforts of Mayor Lahat and my mother. It still remains a very viable institution today, helping many underprivileged and abused students. My mother's dedication was recognized by the community when the names of my parents were affixed to a new community center. I recall traveling to Israel for the dedication ceremony as a teenager and listening to my father explain to me privately:

"I don't usually like for them to put my name on places I give money to," he counseled me. "I don't like it for two reasons. First of all, it's not the Jewish way. The highest form of charity, tzedakah, is when both the giver and the recipient don't know who the other is. The other reason is if they put your name on a building, once you're dead they take it off and replace it with somebody else's name. But I made an exception here because of your mother. She put so much hard work and energy into making this happen, I just couldn't say no when they came and asked me if they could do it."

Sure enough, my father's prophetic words came to pass. The community fathers did, in fact, recently remove my parents' names from the building. When I inquired about it, I was assured that this was done only for renovation purposes and there was no intention to permanently replace their names with those of others. Happily, a short time ago I received word that their names had been restored to their appropriate places, hopefully to stay.

The family has continued its support for this community to this day. We were instrumental in setting up an endowment fund at the Fifth Avenue Synagogue that purchased some property near the community center. Thanks to the congregants' contributions to this fund, the synagogue was able to turn the property into a beautiful park, just a short walk from the community center.

Although he respected her dedication, my father was not at all supportive of my mother's involvement in secular Jewish causes. His focus was on supporting the religious institutions, schools and synagogues, that were entrusted with passing our faith heritage on to the next generation. Myrtle would typically wait until Henry was out of the house before she took off for the UJA office. She also did not leave UJA literature lying around the house. She was not doing her charity work behind his back, exactly. But she simply did not wish to provoke any unnecessary arguments. The inverse was not the case, however. My mother was always extremely supportive of all of my father's philanthropic efforts.

It was in this way, via input from both of my parents, that my attitudes about the importance of philanthropy were shaped. Through my father I gained a deep appreciation for the sacred side of Judaism, while through my mother I was exposed to our culture's more secular dimension. I feel fortunate that I was provided with both sides since it allowed me to maintain a stabilizing balance in my own philanthropy—directing support to both religious and to social welfare causes. I consider them both equally vital to the future of the Jewish people.

Even though my mother never attended college, she was a brilliant writer. And I mean that in the literal sense. She had a beautiful cursive handwriting. I recall sitting with her on Sunday afternoons, going over my essays in preparation for school the following day. She would write a sentence in her gliding script and then I would copy it onto my paper. It was my work, but with a little help from my mom.

While my father never graduated from high school, he managed to climb to great heights of achievement thanks to his own hard work and tenacity. He brought these same skills to bear when pursuing his communal activities. Given his stature in both the business realm and the philanthropic world, my parents would often host dignitaries at our home for dinner. The meal would be served by members of our live-in staff and unlike some parents might have opted to do, my folks never banished us from the dinner table when VIPs were invited. In fact, they would always encourage us to join them and participate in the conversation. Whether it was the mayor from an Israeli town, an Ambassador from another country, businessmen, writers, musicians, old friends, new friends or just extended family, we were always made to feel welcome.

I recall how, over a time period spanning fifteen years, my parents would host a huge Passover Seder each year at Grossinger's, the famous Catskill resort. We would all be called to the table to begin the service, but while the men would take their seats, many of the women would linger behind in the lobby, waiting for my mother to regally descend the staircase. They were excited to see what she was wearing, and she never disappointed them.

While it was Grossinger's for Passover in the spring of every year, we did not go there during the summer months. This was because we owned a sprawling thirty-five acre estate in scenic Ossining, New York and spent our summer holidays there. It was jointly owned by my father, his brother A.P. Hirsh and General Instrument CEO, Mike Benedict. It was a truly beautiful, fully appointed facility with a tennis court, a two-hole golf course, and arguably the largest privately owned swimming pool in New York, all situated on perfectly manicured grounds with formal gardens and groomed pathways connecting the residences. It also boasted a greenhouse that provided vegetables all summer long. My uncle A.P. and his family lived in the large manor house while we lived in a slightly smaller abode with a great view of the Hudson River. The Benedicts also lived in another house on the grounds.

There was one more structure on the estate. It was originally intended to be a guest house, but my father decided to use it for something special. He converted it into a *shteibel*, a small synagogue used for prayer and occasional *Shabbos* services. Of course, this sometimes presented a challenge. In order to hold a service involving the Torah, it is necessary to convene a *minyan* (quorum) of at least ten Jewish men over Bar Mitzvah age. If there were only nine or fewer present, the Torah could not be opened and the service could not take place. While all three of the property owners (Hirsch, Hirsch and Benedict) were Jewish, they at times had to scramble to come up with the needed additional seven. Usually, guests would visit over the weekends and the *minyan* threshold could be reached. But sometimes, they were forced to call the cops. My father had made friends with Officer Sam, a Jewish motorcycle policeman who patrolled the area. If they were a man short for a *minyan*, Henry would ring up Officer Sam and within half an hour, he would be there, *davening* (praying) in my father's private synagogue.

Being a police officer in Ossining was something of a distinction because the town served as home to the infamous federal prison known as Sing-Sing. This fact came into play when, in June, 1953, the so-called "atomic spies," Julius and Ethel Rosenberg, were executed via the electric chair. I know this sounds like a scene from a movie, but I swear I remember the lights dimming in our house as the switch was thrown. Some claimed that the Rosenberg's were victims of antisemitism and, had they not been Jews, they would not have received such a harsh punishment. Historians today, however, agree that the Rosenbergs were truly guilty of espionage that channeled secrets about the US nuclear program into Soviet hands and it was this information that enabled the Russians to construct nuclear weapons that greatly exacerbated the Cold War threat of worldwide destruction.

But such worries were not on our minds during those lazy summers of my admittedly privileged youth. The place still shimmers in my memory as a sort of private country club. In fact, when they put it on the market in 1955, it was sold to an actual country club. Our family had gotten tired of the two-hour drive to Ossining and found a summer spot closer to New York City.

The one over-arching theme that identified my father, from the Ossining estate to his office in Maspeth, was his unwavering belief in the price of privilege. Whether it was helping refugees escape from terror in Europe or writing a check to a needy orphanage in Israel, my father paid that price often, and alway in a modest non-public manner. He had been afforded many blessings thanks to his hard work; thanks to the liberty and opportunities he found in America; and thanks to the grace of God. Such blessings came with a price tag that my father never hesitated to pay. These were values that I absorbed in my youth from both my parents and that have served me well throughout my life.

CHAPTER FIVE
MY FATHER'S HOUSE OF WORSHIP

The Fifth Avenue Synagogue

"For my house shall be called a house of prayer for all nations."

— Isaiah 56

As recounted elsewhere in this book, my father, Henry Hirsch, achieved spectacular financial success despite the Great Depression that held the American economy in its grip throughout the 1930's. One aspect to which he would often point as being responsible for his "Only in America" rise to riches was his close affinity to Judaism.

The more successful my father became, the more involved he became in Jewish affairs—both communal and spiritual. During the first five years of my life, when we lived in Lawrence, Long Island, my parents would, for example, host the *Kiddush* reception every

Saturday after the *Shabbos* services at our local synagogue. By the time we left Lawrence after the war and moved to Manhattan, Henry was already well-known as a serious Jew who knew how to direct his generosity towards the synagogue. Hence, the leadership of the various congregations that dotted New York's Upper East Side soon came knocking on the door. After conducting his due diligence, my father decided to join Congregation Zichron Ephraim which is today known as the Park East Synagogue on 67th Street.

As recounted earlier, Zichron Ephraim was founded in the 1890's as an Orthodox synagogue intended to counter-balance the rising number of Reform synagogues that had popped up to accomodate an influx of well-to-do German Jews who had moved into the area in order to flee the wave of recently-arrived *"Oesten-Juden"* (Jews from Eastern Europe). Joining with notable congregants such as author Herman Wouk, my parents and their cohorts, Leib and Hermann Merkin, led the synagogue through a period of rapid growth through the 1950's. But in 1958 the synagogue was rocked by one of Judaism's most venerated traditions. Divine Disagreement. It is this tradition of dispute and dissatisfaction that has accounted for the creation of almost every new synagogue in America. A group of congregants are unhappy with the this or that religious practice and decide to form a splinter group and thereby go on to found a new congregation.

This point was driven home to me in a most likely apocryphal story my father would often recount. It seems that the *"Alte Rebbe"* (old rabbi) was visited in his sickbed by a delegation of lay leaders from his synagogue. The president of the congregation spoke first.

"Dear Rabbi, we apologize for bothering you, but a matter of such urgency has come up that we have no choice but to turn to you in order to settle the matter." The old man's eyes opened as he nodded for the president to continue.

"Here's the problem. During every *Shabbos* service, when we get to the recitation of the *Sh'ma* (Judaism's holy creed declaration), half the congregation stands up while the other half stays seated.

The half who stand up yells at the sitters to stand and the sitters yell at the standers to sit down. It's a mess. So we decided to come to you to learn what is the tradition. I, for one, believe that you should stand. Am I correct, Rabbi?"

The feeble clergyman struggled to prop himself up on one elbow and managed to say, as he waved a finger back and forth: "That is not the tradition."

"Aha," blurted the Chairman of the Men's Club. "You see. I was right. The tradition is for us to remain seated during the *Sh'ma.*"

Again, the rabbi sat up a bit and muttered: "No. That also is not the tradition."

The three leaders looked puzzled at this and finally the head of the Women's Auxiliary spoke up: "But, Rabbi. It must be one way or the other. If we don't get this resolved we will continue to have complete chaos with half the congregation yelling and screaming at the other half all the time."

The rabbi sat up at this and announced: "Yes! THAT is the tradition."

The cause of the dispute at Congregation Zichron Ephraim was not about when to sit, but rather where to sit. When my father joined the synagogue, the area for women to sit during services was in an upstairs balcony. As the congregation grew and wished to appeal to younger, more liberal families, it was decided to permit women to be seated on the first floor as well as the balcony. Of course, men and women would still need to be separated via a partition wall, called a *mechitza*, that ran down the middle of the sanctuary. The purpose of the *mechitza* was to keep the worshippers focused on their prayers and avoid the distraction caused by a clear view of the opposite sex. Of course this introduced the perplexing problem of how high to make the *mechitza*. Should it only block the view when the congregants were seated or should it be tall enough so no glimpses may be gained even while standing? My father and his small crew argued vehemently for the taller partition, but in the end they lost the battle of the barrier. There was only one thing to do. Start your own synagogue.

Actually, by this point, my father was not particularly happy at Zirchon Ephraim and felt that belonging to a synagogue in a more upscale, secure neighborhood would benefit our family. He was not motivated in this regard by any sense of snobbery, but because he always fought to deliver the best of everything to his family. So he, along with a couple of his building buddies, went shopping for some suitable synagogue space. They found the perfect spot on East 62nd Street, between Fifth and Madison Avenues.

When my father's group broke away in 1958 to found what would become the Fifth Avenue Synagogue, it was not only other lay leaders who joined him. The spinoff group also included the synagogue's cantor. Cantor Bernard Bloomstein, known as Barney, was a close friend of my father's and when it came time to jump ship, Barney was definitely on board. In addition to chanting the liturgical prayers during services—on a strictly volunteer basis, by the way—Barney was also a successful businessman. He owned and operated a kosher canned food operation. My father had often assisted Cantor Barney in his business ventures and hence had earned the *hazzan's* (cantor's) loyalty and deep friendship.

My father, Henry Hirsch, is listed as the visionary founding chairman of the Fifth Avenue Synagogue, while my mother, Myrtle was the founder of the Women's Club. They, along with the Merkin family, sought to create an institution that would embody the idealized values of Orthodox Judaism. But synagogues in those days fulfilled more than a spiritual mission. These founders wished to create a synagogue that would appeal to modern Jews who were immersed in the life of contemporary America. They wished to create an aesthetically-pleasing ambience that would provide space for social, educational and cultural activities as well as prayer.

Jewish tradition is guided by the principle of *Torah im Derech Eretz*, which translates as "Scripture and the way of the Land." It is the title of a well-known 19th century book by Rabbi Samson Raphael Hirsch (no relation) and promotes the idea that a synagogue must go beyond serving as merely a venue for *t'fillah* (prayer) and stretch to serve the educational and social needs of its congregants. It is this foundation upon which my father and the others built the Fifth Avenue Synagogue.

For the position of chief rabbi, the group attracted no less of a figure than the Chief Rabbi of Ireland, Dr. Immanuel Jakobovits. After leaving Fifth Avenue, Rabbi Jakobovits went on to serve as the Chief Rabbi of England, where he was knighted in 1981 and, in 1988, entered the House of Lords as Baron Jakobovits. Rabbi Jakobovits was succeeded by Dr. Rabbi Emanuel Rackman, the future Chancellor of Bar Ilan University in Israel.

There was an interrum period after the group left Zichron Ephraim but before the building on Fifth Avenue was ready for occupancy. During this time the new group met at the facility operated by the New York Board of Rabbis. The founders retained the services of noted architect Percival Goodman to design their new home. A home they wished to become a New York City landmark location. Goodman was known as the "Father of the Modern Synagogue," having designed more than fifty Jewish houses of worship during the mid-twentieth century. He was described by his peers as the leading theorist of modern synagogue design and was, by all accounts, the most prolific architect in Jewish history. While not originally an observant Jew, he eventually devoted his life to creating magnificent Jewish spiritual edifices. "I was an agnostic who was converted by Hitler," he would often quip.

Goodman's primary challenge was constructing a synagogue with a large sanctuary on a lot that was very deep but much too narrow. His solution required that he borrow a layout from the Sephardic tradition which placed the *bimah* (altar) and the ark in a central area and featured facing sections of worshippers. Of course, the layout included an *Ezrat Nashim*, the Court of Women in the balcony. The ingenious floor plan has been admired ever since, not only for its inventive use of space, but because, as an Orthodox synagogue, it is wholly *Halakhically* (legally) compliant.

One of the reasons my father selected the Fifth Avenue location for his new synagogue was its proximity to our home, only ten short blocks away. During those days, Henry would stop in at the construction site every morning to oversee the progress, arriving at his office at Welbilt well after ten am. I still recall accompanying him every Sunday morning and walking the ten blocks to meet with Barney Bloomstein at the construction site. While the finished building remains a striking piece of post-modern architecture to this day, it was not to everyone's liking. There is a scene in the 1986 Woody Allen film, HANNAH AND HER SISTERS, that pans across the synagogue's face as a voice-over actor criticizes its architectural incongruity. "That's disgusting. That's really terrible," he says, clearly upset that the building disrupts the consistent facades of the rest of the block.

Despite such parochial snobbery, the Fifth Avenue Synagogue became a venue for many of the community's cultural and even athletic activities. In a nod to me, and as a tactic designed to attract young men to the synagogue, my father had insisted that the building include a full-court basketball facility on the sixth floor. It was later converted to a nursery pre-school.

My earliest recollection of attending a function at the new synagogue was my sister Carole's wedding which was, in fact, the very first social event ever held there. Today, the Fifth Avenue Synagogue is home to a thriving congregation and is often a stop for visiting Jewish dignitaries. Nobel Laureate Elie Wiesel was a frequent worshipper who, like conductor Leonard Bernstein—who often attended during the High Holidays—commented that he was attracted by the synagogue's celebrated cantor, Joseph Malovany.

Possessor of a powerful spinto tenor voice, Cantor Malovany was originally hired by my father, and as of this writing, continues to serve as the synagogue's world-renowned cantor. Writer Herman Wouk, author of THE CAINE MUTINY and THE WINDS OF WAR, and one of the synagogue's founders in the 1950's, retained his affiliation till his death at age 103 in May of 2019.

My mother's role in the establishment and growth of the Fifth Avenue Synagogue cannot be overstated. Listed as one of the synagogue's founders, Myrtle's stylish elegance and keen fashion sense served to attract the finest ladies through its doors. Over the years, she served in almost every capacity from Board member to president of the Women's Club to the director of programming. It is no overstatement to say that the Fifth Avenue Synagogue was a shared passion that served to solidify and strengthen my parents' marriage.

Although he was too modest a man to receive any recognition during his lifetime for it, it should be noted here that the Fifth Avenue Synagogue would never have gotten off the ground without a deep financial commitment made by Henry Hirsch. The synagogue's role today, as Manhattan's pre-eminent Jewish house of worship, was envisioned by its founders early on. They knew that creating a synagogue of such scope and breadth would require substantial funding. To his enduring credit, my father quietly secured both the construction loan and the permanent mortgage for the synagogue with his personal negotiable assets. The notes were paid off in time, and his collateral unencumbered. When, years later, I inquired about why he was willing to take on such risk, he told me: "Richard, that was the best investment I ever made."

At the occasion of the Fifth Avenue's Synagogue's 25th anniversary in 1983, Wouk was invited to offer a few words of reflection about the rededication of this beloved house of prayer that he and my father had created. Here are a few of his eloquent words:

"And so, week in and week out, year in and year out, the Fifth Avenue Synagogue has been diffusing tradition in the elegant heart of New York as Jewish men and women have been *davening* and learning in the old way. The members and the visitors have become, over the years, a Who's Who of World Jewry.

The pattern is single and clear: Torah Judaism is stepping forth into new times and assuming new leadership tasks. That is, I suggest, the secret of secrets of our tradition; that in all times and places, re-dedication works."

Richard L. Hirsch

Photo Album
Part I

Richard L. Hirsch

Sempre Avanti!

My brother, David (l) and me (r) with Olympic speed-skating champion, Irving Jaffe at Grossinger's.

(l to r) My father, Henry sch, actor William Bendix, and my mother, Myrtle Hirsch. One of the many celebrities with whom my parents were friendly.

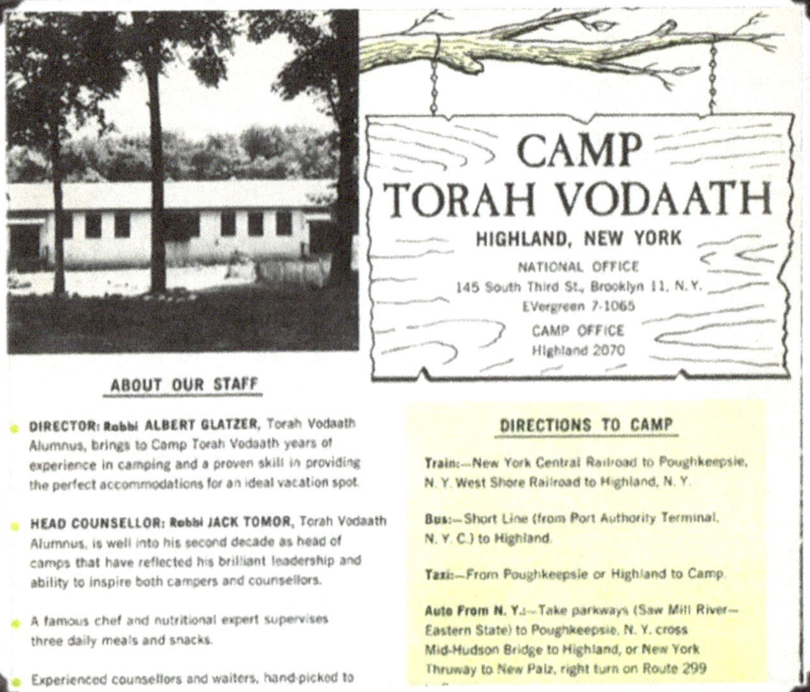

*Newspaper ad for
Camp Torah Vodaath.*

*My father, Henry Hirsch,
at his desk.*

Sempre Avanti!

With my brother, David, playing doubles tennis at Grossinger's.

Family Portrait.
(l-r) Standing: My sister, Carole; me.
Seated: My parents, Henry and Myrtle Hirsch; my brother, David.

At a Grossinger's sporting event. Top row (r-l): My father, Henry Hirsch; me; Dorothy Neustater; my mother, Myrtle Hirsch.

My mother, Myrtle Hirsch (r) and my father, Henry Hirsch in a British Bobby outfit attending a costume party.

Sempre Avanti!

(l-r) Me; my mother, Myrtle; my brother, David; and my sister, Carole.

My mother, Myrtle Hirsch, a long-time baseball fan, makes front-page news, along with the Brooklyn Dodgers in the October 5, 1955 edition of the New York Daily Mirror.

My mother, Myrtle, dressed for a a formal evening.

(l-r) Top row: My uncle, A.P. Hirsch; an unnamed Welbilt executive; my aunt, Mary Hirsch.
Seated: My mother, Myrtle Hirsch; my father, Henry Hirsch; unnamed Welbilt executives attending an industry dinner.

Sempre Avanti!

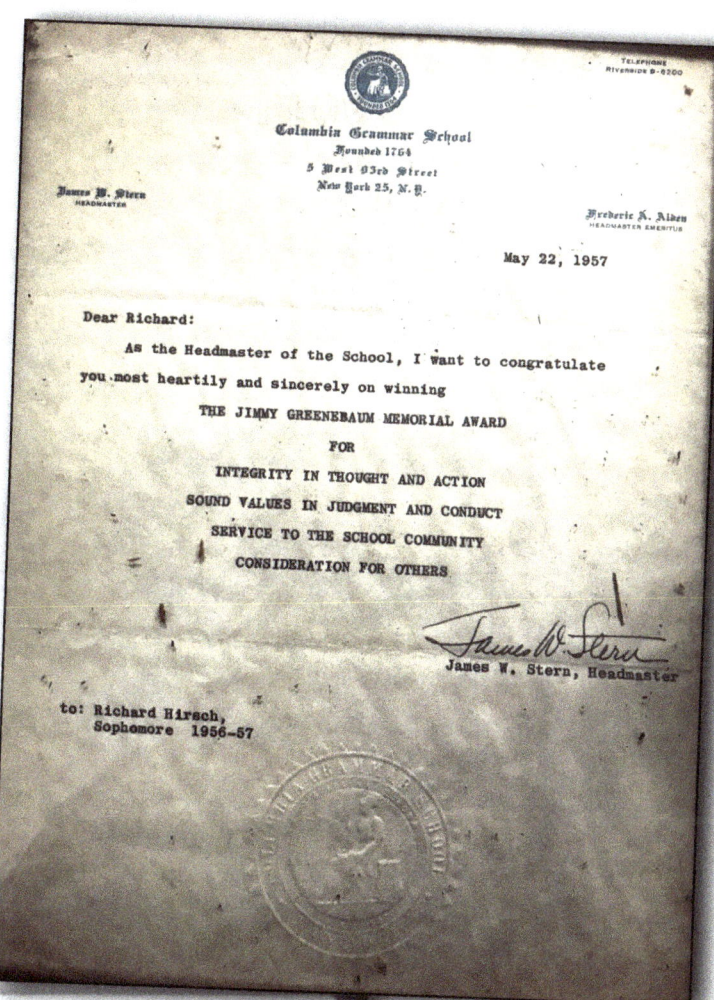

> Columbia Grammar School
> Founded 1764
> 5 West 93rd Street
> New York 25, N.Y.
>
> James W. Stern, HEADMASTER
> Frederic A. Alden, HEADMASTER EMERITUS
>
> May 22, 1957
>
> Dear Richard:
>
> As the Headmaster of the School, I want to congratulate you most heartily and sincerely on winning
>
> THE JIMMY GREENEBAUM MEMORIAL AWARD
>
> FOR
>
> INTEGRITY IN THOUGHT AND ACTION
> SOUND VALUES IN JUDGMENT AND CONDUCT
> SERVICE TO THE SCHOOL COMMUNITY
> CONSIDERATION FOR OTHERS
>
> James W. Stern, Headmaster
>
> to: Richard Hirsch,
> Sophomore 1956-57

Notice of my receipt of the highly prestigious Jimmy Greenebaum Memorial Award I received in high school.

Dancing with my delighted mother, Myrtle Hirsch, at Grossinger's.

GENERAL ORGANIZATION CABINET

Left to Right, First row: Claire Davis, Jonathan Lyons, Allan Mann, Bill Greilsheimer, Marilyn Seitman.
Top row: Jerry Wiesen, Bill Shonbrun, Donald Weckstein, Richard Hirsch, Mike Tarant, Bruce Brown.

From my high school yearbook. The General Organization Cabinet. I'm standing third from the right.

Columbia Grammar High School Graduating Class.

On the phone at Welbilt. I became president of Welbilt in 1971 upon the retirement of my father. I directed the restructuring process that resulted in the company's turnaround.

My ex-wife, Joyce, holding our son, Larry Hirsch, of blessed memory.

Family portrait taken in the foyer of my parents, Henry and Myrtle's, apartment. Early 1980s.

Back Row (l-r): Joyce's step-father, Sam Davis; me; son, Daniel; brother-in-law, Mickey Friedman; Debbie Friedman's husband, Mark Cooper; nephew, Jonny Friedman; brother, David; Rochelle's father, Herbert Cohen; Mickey Friedman's father, Hy Friedman.

In chairs (l-r): Joyce's mother, Emma Davis; my wife, Joyce; sister, Carole Friedman; mother, Myrtle Hirsch; father, Henry Hirsch; Rochelle, David's wife; Rochelle's mother, Terry Cohen; Mickey's mother, Sylvia Friedman.

On floor (l-r): daughter, Michelle; neice, Debbie Friedman; son, Adam; nephew, Jeffrey Hirsch; nephew, Jason Hirsch; neice Lisa Friedman.

Sempre Avanti!

With fellow board member, Danny Baldinger at Maimonides Medical Center celebration at Plaza Hotel in New York City.

y parents, Henry and Myrtle Hirsch, at home.

(l-r) Standing: Carole and Mickey Friedman; Rochelle and David Hirsch. Seated: me and Joyce Hirsch; Henry and Myrtle Hirsch.

A perfect caricature of me. The voice balloon reads: "Joyce, I can't figure it out — I have this back pain that just doesn't quit"

Gail and Ephie Propp. Long-standing friends of the family.

I'm gonna need a bigger boat!

(l-r) David Hirsch; unidentified man; Rochelle Hirsch; me; Judith Kidron, first principal of Mifton Alon.

As chairman of Maimonides Medical Center.

My favorite family portrait. (l-r) Standing: our son, Daniel; my ex-wife, Joyce; our son, Adam; me; our daughter, Michelle.

I thought that planting a garden would help me to relax. This was the only time I ever went in it.

With former Israeli Prime Minister, Ehud Olmert.

Astride Sunny, who is making me look good.

CHAPTER SIX
THE MAKING OF A MANAGER

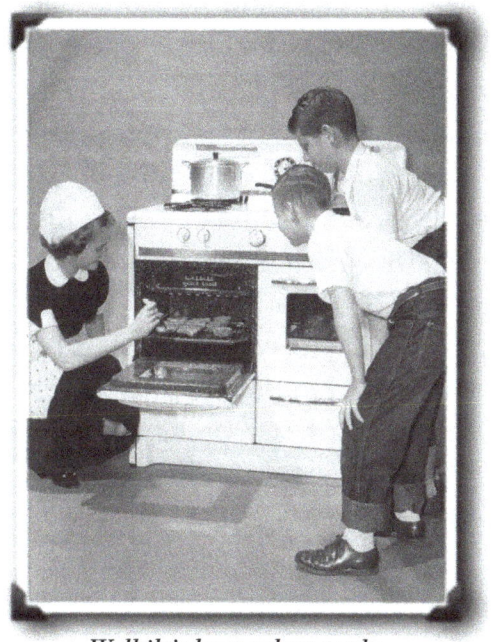

Welbilt's best salespeople.
My sister, Carole; my brother, David; and me in the early 1950s.

"Giving people self-confidence is by far the most important thing you can do. Because then they will act."

— Jack Welch

As I recounted earlier, after my two-week post-graduation hiatus, I went straight to work at the Welbilt shipping department learning how to package kitchen equipment properly for the journey from the factory to the restaurant. After a suitable amount of time, I was transferred to the sales department, then to the finance department, and eventually to every area within the company. I stayed at each assignment just long enough to gain an in-depth understanding of how each one operated and fit in to the overall corporate structure. It wasn't merely observation. It was learning by doing. My tenure at each stop was essentially up to me. At a certain point, at each department, I would approach the person in charge and say: "I've got this. Time for me to move on."

If I was treated with any sort of deference by company employees during this orientation period, I was too busy to notice. I actually got along very well with everyone, although I noticed a systemic problem that was pervasive throughout the company. There seemed to be a great deal of friction between departments. Each was plagued by a sense of isolation and constant struggle for more authority and autonomy. There were petty "turf wars" between department heads that served to the detriment of the smooth efficiency that we needed. After a few months, I came to understand how this lack of cooperation between departments was taking a toll on company earnings. As a result of the year and a half I spent learning the lay of the land, I made it my first priority to try and restore a sense of unity and cooperation as part of our corporate culture. I am pleased to say, that thanks to the guidance of one very extraordinary individual, I was able to accomplish this feat. I will introduce you to him in the next chapter.

Once I ascended to the top management level at Welbilt, I discovered that the core company was no longer being run by its founders, my father and his brother, A.P. Hirsch. A.P. was heading up the associated real estate development company, Padar, while my dad, as mentioned, was heavily focused on his philanthropic activities. Occasionally, he took an interest in one of the smaller companies Welbilt had acquired. One such company was Unagusta.

It was shortly after completing my orientation that my father approached me and instructed me to pack a bag. "We're going to Chicago." This was my very first business trip, but instead of going on behalf of one of Welbilt's kitchen equipment companies, Dad and I would be representing Unagusta, a maker of fine furniture, that Welbilt had acquired in 1960. The trade show was to be held at the old Merchandise Mart that was owned by Joseph P. Kennedy, the father of the then recently martyred president of the United

States. We were there to make deals with furniture retailers who distributed the Unagusta product line. One of the largest was Macy's in New York.

Unagusta Furniture Manufacturing Company—named after a famed local Indian chief—was founded in the 1920's in Hazelton, located in the heart of North Carolina's furniture region. Owned and operated by R.L. Prevost and his four sons, the factory burned to the ground in 1955. It was rebuilt in nearby Waynesville and was known for its high-quality bedroom suites by the time it was acquired by Welbilt. Unagusta was a problem child for Welbilt from the very beginning. The company's major claim to fame was its use of a proprietary veneer finish on its household furnishing products. But the stuff didn't hold up. Dealers and retailers were constantly complaining to us about customers who were dissatisfied as the finish quickly wore off, marring the beauty of their beds, dressers and dining room tables.

Because of these issues and because our company was fundamentally a commercial kitchen equipment-maker and knew little about managing a furniture business, Unagusta became a money loser and a cash drain. During the 1960's, it was supported by Padar, the family real estate entity, where it did not fare much better.

Unagusta became the first of the consumer goods companies I sold off after becoming president of Welbilt in 1971 at age 29. The company had reached a peak revenue mark a few years earlier at just under $57 million in sales. But by the time I took the helm, it had started losing money; a cash drain that took me three more years to staunch. During 1971 and 1972 Unagusta had racked up $6 million in losses. We managed to sell it for $5 million in 1973 to Lea Furniture as part of a major shift out of the consumer market. I realized that we could not survive if we continued to make and market consumer goods. Two more consumer product companies were also scrapped in 1974. Through downsizing and consolidation, I was able to return Welbilt to profitability within five years of my assuming the presidency. Lea Furniture continued to produce the Unagusta brand until closing its doors in 2014. Unagusta furnishings may be found today advertised at estate auctions and are considered to be highly prized for their quality.

Back at home, Joyce had secured a rewarding job as an elementary school teacher in Manhattan. She was a dedicated and devoted educator but left teaching after the birth of our first son, Larry, in 1967. Joyce was also an outstanding bridge player and got me involved to the point that most of the evenings when I was at home during those years were spent with another couple around a card table.

During the 1950's, Welbilt had acquired another consumer products company, the Culver City, California-based stove maker called Western-Holly. Their stoves bore a distinctive feature: a round oven window that resembled a ship porthole. The company soon became my pet project. One of the reasons that attracted me on business trips to Western-Holly was the opportunity I had to hop over to Las Vegas whenever I was there. For several years I was traveling to Culver City at least every other month.

Once I had taken care of my business responsibilities at Western-Holly, I would hop a flight to Vegas for the weekend. This was during the glory days of Frankie, Dino, and Sammy, known as the Rat Pack, and I would often find myself aboard a commuter aircraft with one of the unholy crew en route to a Vegas gig. When the plane took off, so did the party.

Once I reached Vegas, I was the guest of Jack Entratter, the vice president of the Rat Pack's home base, the Sands Hotel. These were the years just before Howard Hughes snatched up the Sands along with multiple Las Vegas casino properties. It was Entratter who handled the bookings and signed Frank Sinatra for his Las Vegas debut in 1953. The Sands was featured prominently in the original Ocean's 11 movie and was the site of Jerry Lewis and Dean Martin's final performance together.

My connection to Jack Entratter came through his former business associate, Jules Podell. Podell lived in our building at 910 Fifth Avenue and became good friends with my father. Podell was the "official" owner of the famed Copa Cabana night spot, where such luminaries as Danny Thomas, Pat Cooper, Martin & Lewis and the Supremes had made their New York City debuts. The Copa, as it is still known to this day, opened in 1940 on East 60th Street. It was owned by mob boss, Frank Costello, who originally needed a front man to put his name on the lease and obtain a liquor license. Costello retained a well-known press agent, Monte Proser, for this role and then put Podell on the scene to look after Costello's interests. When the club was facing a racketeering investigation in 1948, Costello got rid of Proser, who had a police record, and made Podell the official "owner" of the Copa Cabana. Podell's right hand man was Jack Entratter and when Costello bought into the newly-built Sands Hotel Casino, he moved Jack from the Copa to the Sands.

I was given a royal treatment at the Sands by Mr. Entratter's casino manager, Nick Kelly, whenever I took one of these weekend junkets to Sin City. The finest meals, luxury suites, and free tickets to the best shows in town...with only one caveat. No gambling. I recall my first visit when Mr. Kelly took me aside and told me in confidence: "Look, Richard, Mr. Podell and your dad are buddies and he told your dad that he'd take care of you whenever you come to Vegas. So Mr. Entratter wanted me to ask you to stay away from the casino. He told me that you can have the run of the joint, just stay away from the tables? Got it?"

I told him that I understood, and, for the most part, I was as good as my word. I wasn't much of a gambler anyway. At the most, I might have spent fifteen minutes at a craps table. So, one might ask, what did I do all day in Las Vegas if I wasn't gambling? Believe it or not, I went sight seeing. I went on bus trips to Hoover Dam and Lake Mead, visited the Grand Canyon, and Death Valley National Park.

The Sands was acquired by Howard Hughes in 1967 and that's when my weekends jaunts came to a stop. But the memory of those days and nights in "Vintage Vegas" linger to this day.

Although Joyce would never accompany me on these "business mixed with pleasure" trips, she knew that I could be trusted and I never gave her reason to think otherwise. She was working very hard as a teacher and my demanding schedule meant that we did not see very much of each other. Joyce was raised in an assimilated Jewish family that did not observe the Jewish dietary laws known as *Kashruth*. Nevertheless, she had no difficulty in adapting to a kosher kitchen once we were married. She was never a religious person and was more aligned with the secular and cultural dimension of Judaism. Yet this difference between us was never an issue. We made it all work smoothly starting before our children came along.

When Welbilt went public in 1959, our family retained controlling interest, with the shares being split among the various family branches. Although I was not officially named CEO until my father's retirement in 1971, within two years of my joining the company, I was being consulted about every major decision and was soon at the helm and serving as the de facto president. With the company's founders having stepped back from their leadership roles, it fell to me to provide the corporate guidance and report to the stockholders through the Board. By the time I assumed the title of CEO, I had actually been running the company for more than five years. Nevertheless, I was written up in the media at that point for being the youngest CEO of a Fortune 500 publicly-traded company. That record stood through 1995 when Dell Computer joined the Fortune 500 and its founder, Michael Dell, at age 27, became the youngest CEO ever. I believe that record still stands today in 2020.

Although my father and uncle offered some support, I was not able to look to them for much guidance as I struggled in my role as the president of a company that was bleeding money. But evidently, G-d was looking out for me and allowed me to fall under the wing of perhaps the most influential person I have ever known. As recounted in the following chapter, Moses "Monte" Shapiro was a family friend who soon became something more than my mentor. In many ways he became my messiah.

CHAPTER SEVEN
THE FULL MONTE

In my Welbilt CEO office with director, Moses (Monte) Shapiro.

"Organize. Deputize. Supervise. That's management."
— Moses "Monte" Shapiro

It's not clear who first said it, but an oft-repeated adage goes: "If you think that you're the smartest person in the room, you're in the wrong room." The point being is that if you surround yourself with intellectual inferiors, you will never experience significant growth. I'm happy to say that for many years I was at little risk of making this mistake because often the room in question was the boardroom at Welbilt and there was never a question about who was the smartest person in the room. It wasn't me. All agreed it was Moses Shapiro, known to one and all as Monte.

From the time of his retirement as CEO of electronics giant, General Instrument, till his death in 1990, Monte Shapiro helped to guide the rising fortunes of Welbilt during my tenure as CEO. My parents had known Monte since the 1940's when he had served on the War Labor Board. He was a frequent visitor to our home in Ossining and I recall how my father spoke of him with hushed reverence for his brilliance when it came to business. "There's nobody smarter that's ever sat at our dinner table," I recall him telling me.

Because of this high regard for Monte's intelligence and integrity, I began consulting with him while he was still at General Instrument. This was shortly after I took over as CEO of Welbilt and was struggling to turn around a company that had been losing money for five years. His counsel and common sense were invaluable to me and by the time I offered Monte a seat on our board following his retirement in 1977, I had succeeded, with his help, in turning the corner to profitability through divestiture and consolidation. At this point, Welbilt was poised and ready for growth and that's where Monte really shined.

Monte had been with General Instrument since shortly after World War II. In the early 1950's, he abandoned his career as a labor negotiator and joined the management team of one of his clients, a maker of radio transformers that eventually became General Instrument. By 1960 he had become CEO and launched a campaign of growth via the acquisition of smaller New York-based electronics firms, eventually growing into a huge technology conglomerate by the time he became chairman in 1969. It was at this point that he moved the company into a number of high-tech industries such as silicon transistor and semiconductor manufacturing. His timing could not have been better. It was General Instrument in the 1970's that leveraged semiconductor technology to create the set-top boxes used in the skyrocketing new industry of Cable TV. General Instrument owned the market for such devices for decades after Monte's retirement in 1977.

Monte was a devout believer in growth through acquisition. Welbilt, likewise, had been gobbling up smaller manufacturing concerns since the 1930's, although some of those companies proved to be more of a liability. I recognized that if we were ever again to go on an acquisition expedition, we would need to do so cautiously and wisely. Monte was just the man to head up the expedition. He was incredible when it came to analyzing a company's fundamental financials and scrutinizing its product line. There was not a single acquisition made during those years that did not receive Monte's seal of approval.

Just having Monte on our board was viewed as a plus by our directors, stockholders and executives. Monte, from his office in the General Motors Building, was considered one of luminary American industrialists of that era, alongside such figures as Jack Welch, Lee Iacocca and Gordon Moore. Although Monte was originally a lawyer, he was greatly loved by our company's engineers. The reason was his hands-on style. Many board members regard their board seats as an honorary position and leave the day-to-day operations to the management team. Not so with Monte. His first task upon assuming his seat was to meet individually with every department—financial, product development, sales, etc.—in order to educate himself about the company's operations. He became something of a father figure to the engineers, at least the competent ones. Those who did not meet his performance expectations understood that their careers at Welbilt could be cut short by Mr. Shapiro. Whenever such a situation arose, Monte would consult with me about letting someone go. I usually heeded his advice and would agree to the discharge, although he always insisted that it was my responsibility to deliver the bad news to the employee in person.

Monte commanded the loyalty of our engineers and our executives through a combination of fear and respect. More than anything else, they respected his unwavering work ethic. One that he expected everyone around him to similarly observe. One of the company's top engineers worked very closely with Monte on product design. Late one winter's evening, as they were working furiously to meet a deadline, Monte suggested that they knock off and return in the morning.

"But, Mr. Shapiro, tomorrow is Christmas Day. I'll be celebrating with my family tomorrow morning," pointed out the engineer.

"Oh, I see," Monte responded. "Well can we work on it in the afternoon, then?"

Under Monte's tutelage I began to hone my own work habits as I emulated the values that he embodied. I'll never forget the day I rushed into his office fifteen minutes late for a meeting . Monte was reading the Wall Street Journal.

"Sorry, I'm late, Monte," I blurted taking a chair. "There was a traffic tie up on the highway." I'll never forget his next words, spoken without looking up from his newspaper:

"Tell me, Richie, what makes you think that your time is more valuable than mine?"

I was never late for an appointment with Monte again.

Monte believed that there were two types of people in the world: concurrent and consecutive. He preferred the former and taught me the value of being someone who could handle multiple duties at the same time, or what we now call "multi-tasking." He explained that during his career as a labor negotiator he was called upon to move repeatedly from various rooms, each containing a different party to the dispute. He had to deal with them all at the same time as opposed to doing so serially or one at a time. By learning how to juggle lots of balls in the air at one time, Monte became adept at the art of concurrency, a skill he used to great advantage when building General Instrument.

It was Monte's influence that prompted me to designate the name Concurrent Industries Group (C.I.G.) to our family investment concern I launched with Larry Gross after leaving Welbilt, and now run by my son, Adam. Based out of New York, C.I.G. invests primarily in private equity and debt financing as well as real estate in a broad range of industries such as foodservice, fitness and manufacturing.

As I point out in my public speaking engagements, it is always better to surround yourself with concurrent rather than consecutive people. Telling the difference is not always obvious, however. I attribute my own working style to my relationship with Monte. At the end of the day, he was an idea guy. He was constantly brainstorming. He would think nothing of waking me with a phone call at 3 am to announce: "Richie, I've got an idea," and proceed to lay it out for me. And I was not the only member of management or engineering who would receive such midnight Monte mind-bursts. In fact, getting a middle of the night call from Monte was something of a badge of honor at Welbilt. It meant he thought enough of you to share his ideas no matter what the time of day or night. To this day, when I visit the Welbilt product development offices in New Port Richey, Florida, to get a peek at some of their latest innovations, I will often hear someone say: "Monte would have loved this."

While Monte was given a modest Director's Fee for his Board service at Welbilt, he never drew a salary or any other compensation for his valuable consultancy work. Monte was one of those rare birds who was not motivated by money. Hence, he did not die a wealthy man. But he did succeed in making others wealthy around him. He also accumulated something he believed was more precious than financial wealth: Respect. Monte was regarded as the most well-respected figure in our industry by all who knew him, including some of the top American industrialists of the 20th century.

Monte's process for evaluating and acquiring companies was nothing short of brilliant. He was a genius when it came to putting deals together. There was another kitchen equipment company we wished to acquire that was composed of seven divisions. We could not accumulate the cash to buy the entire company, so Monte and I evaluated each division and identified the three that had the least prospects for long-term success but had high asset holdings. We bought them and liquidated them immediately, using the cash to buy the remaining four divisions.

When conducting his due diligence in evaluating takeover targets, Monte would often dispatch me to go collect the information he needed. This was primarily due to the fact that he suffered from emphysema and was not permitted to fly. I would bring back financial statements, labor contracts, advertising campaign material, product samples and whatever else he asked for. Monte would then pore over this material and then start making calls to his buddies in the industry. In this way he would be able to get an accurate bead on the company and decide if and how we should attempt to acquire it.

When a takeover target company was identified, our next move was to negotiate favorable terms with the ownership. Often, this would involve sitting down with the company's founders who had more than a financial stake in the takeover. They wished to be assured that whoever took over the company they had built from the ground up would be capable and honorable inheritors of their good name. Having Monte on our side of the table during such negotiations was a big plus. His reputation as a straight shooter and respected captain of industry made it much smoother for us to make our pitch. The owners' pride and proprietary interests were being addressed when they saw they were being acquired by some impressive and high-powered people like Monte.

One of Monte's brightest "bright ideas" had nothing to do with acquisitions or product development. I recall we were chatting in his office about a recently retired engineer—one of Monte's favorites.

"Where do these engineers go when they retire?" he asked me.

"Well, almost all of them go retire to Florida," I replied.

"You know," he said after a moment's thought, "these guys are all still pretty young. They are all talented and experienced. If the only reason they want to leave is because they want to live in Florida, let's build a place in Florida for them." Before I knew it I was on a flight to Tallahassee to scout for locations. I found one in a community just south of Tarpon Springs called New Port Richey and within a year we had opened the Welbilt Engineering Center. This was a simply brilliant idea because it succeeded in our being able to extend the useful life of our engineering talent pool. The facility has grown and remains in use today and now also serves as Welbilt's main corporate headquarters.

I was clearly not the only person who benefited from Monte's mentoring. One of his two sons, Robert, rose to the presidency and chairmanship of agribusiness giant Monsato. As a person, Monte cut an impressive figure. A stocky man with a shock of white hair and matching mustache, Monte radiated respect when he entered a room. He kept his professional and private lives segregated. I barely knew his wife, Barbara Ann, and the only time I saw him interact with her was when she would phone at the end of the day to ask where she should meet him for dinner.

One of the last things Monte did shortly before his death in 1990 was done casually, but it led to a monumental turning point in my life and that of the company. He introduced me to Jerome Kohlberg, Jr. Kohlberg had recently left the highly successful private equity and venture capital firm he had helped found, Kohlberg Kravis Roberts & Co. (KKR) in order to set up his own private equity company, Kohlberg & Co. It was this entity that would enable our family to divest our interest in Welbilt via a leveraged buyout discussed in the following chapters.

My debt to Moses Shapiro is one that can never be fully paid back. He took the world's youngest CEO and shaped me, through his guidance and by example, into a successful business leader. I hope that by telling a bit of his story on the pages of this book, a tiny portion of that debt may be repaid.

Richard L. Hirsch

CHAPTER EIGHT
THE WELBILT STORY PT. I

The thirty ton wooden replica of a Garland kitchen stove that stood at the entrance to the 1893 Columbian Exposition in Chicago.

"Even if you are on the right track, you'll get run over if you just sit there."

— Will Rodgers

They say that "revenge is a dish best served cold." That may be true but when I was in the stove business, we liked to focus on keeping things hot, as the following story demonstrates:

A professional photographer was invited to attend a swanky uptown dinner party. The snooty hostess greeted him and said:

"Oh, I've seen your photographs. They are wonderful. You must have a fantastic camera." Taken aback, the guest said nothing until after the meal, when he approached the hostess and retaliated:

"Oh, that was a wonderful dinner. You must have a fantastic stove."

The story of the company my father and uncle founded in 1929, at the cusp of the Great Depression, has been recounted in industry and financial publications many times over the years and is available online to all who may care to read it. Yet, this narrative would be incomplete without devoting some attention to the company to which I was so intimately devoted during most of my business career. First a bit of history.

Thanks to the acquisition of an older, smaller stove company (the Detroit-Michigan Stove Company) in 1955, the Welbilt Story stretches back even further in time. Back, in fact, to the pre-Civil War era. In 1855 the Soo Locks were opened at Sault Ste. Marie, Michigan. This breakthrough permitted iron ore to be transported quickly by barge from the mineral-rich mines of the Upper Peninsula into Detroit. New access to iron ore led to the establishment of a number of Detroit foundries. Two of these were the Garland Stove Company and the Detroit Stove Works, founded by brothers James and Jeremiah Dwyer in 1861. In 1864, in anticipation of a postwar boom, Detroit Stove acquired Garland and began producing a line of more than 200 varieties of cooking and heating stoves. By the 1880's, stove manufacturing had become Detroit's leading industry. A decade later, Detroit was known as the "Stove Capital of the World." Had the car industry not supplanted this moniker, Detroit today would be known as "Stotown," instead of "Motown," which is short for "Motor Town."

The Garland Stove is perhaps best remembered because of the thirty ton wooden replica of a Garland kitchen stove that stood at the entrance to the 1893 Columbian Exposition in Chicago. The "Big Stove" survived until 2013 when it was struck by lightening while on display at the Michigan State Fairgrounds and was completely destroyed.

As the industry matured, consolidation took place. In 1925, the Detroit Stove Works merged with rival Michigan Stove forming the Detroit-Michigan Stove Company. It was this company that was acquired in 1955 by Welbilt. By this time, Detroit-Michigan was a publicly-traded company. Welbilt inherited its listing on the New York Stock Exchange and became known as the Welbilt Corporation. But how did Welbilt, an enterprise founded by two Jewish first generation immigrants at the onset of the Depression rise to become an industry leader by the mid-1950's? Interestingly, it began because of the Sabbath.

As recounted in Chapter Two, my father, Henry Hirsch, 26 and his older brother, Alexander (A.P.), 31, acquired a small Queens foundry in 1929, two months before the stock market crashed. Our family, that had immigrated from the Austro-Hungarian Empire during the late 19th century found initial financial success in America in the garment (*shmatteh*) business. My grandfather, Louis Hirsch, started out by stitching affordable house dresses in his East Williamsburg home and peddling them door-to-door to Jewish housewives living in nearby tenements. Eventually, he opened a shop on Flushing Avenue, soon followed by several more. By the time his sons became active in the business, the family owned several buildings along Flushing Avenue including one near Maspeth that they leased out to small manufacturing firms.

One such tenant, a maker of enamel products, including the corrugated surfaces used by washboards, was forced to fold as washtubs gave way to washing machines. The family took possession of the facility, thereby making Henry and A.P. the proud owners of a defunct porcelain factory. The family had, for many years, leased space at their 1087 Flushing Avenue building to a company that used mica to manufacture electronic capacitors. This firm, Micamold, made its name by manufacturing mica and paper capacitors for use in the making of consumer radios by companies like Philco and RCA. Micamold would someday go on to become the General Instrument Company, the world's most successful manufacturer of set-top channel-selection boxes for the Cable-TV industry. From their contact with Micamold, the brothers understood that enamel is known for its excellent insulating properties. When deliberating about what to do with their newly-acquired enameling facility, they hit upon an idea that would solve a highly practical problem—a problem that had confounded members of the growing Orthodox Jewish community. How to enjoy a hot lunch on Saturday.

Jews reaching America during the great waves of Eastern European immigration had settled, by the hundreds of thousands, in the New York boroughs of Brooklyn and Queens. Unlike in the *shtetl*s from where they had come, meals in America were not prepared using a wood-burning stove, which also doubled as a source of heat in the winter. Trying to use such stoves would have been impossible in the high-rise tenements in which most Jewish families were housed. Instead, families prepared their meals using steel-fabricated gas stoves and ovens. Lighting a flame on *Shabbos* was forbidden under Jewish law and so such stoves were rendered unusable from sunset each Friday until the following sunset on Saturday.

Eastern European Jews traditionally prepared a hot bean dish known as *cholent* before each *Shabbos*. The name is derived from the French words for warm (chaux) and slow (lent). The dish, prepared in a cast-iron kettle, would be placed into the still-warm oven on Friday night and would remain warm through the following day as the charred wooden embers cooled. The *cholent* would be served —still warm—after *Shabbos* services at mid-day on Saturday. How could this practice be replicated in the New World? My father and uncle thought they had the answer. Build a better stove, outfitted with enamel insulation that would keep the *cholent* warm for 18 hours. Such a stove would need to be built well...or, in their Yiddishized English: Welbilt (pronounced: Velbilt). The Welbilt Stove company began producing such heavily insulated stoves just as the US economy was beginning its descent. Yet, despite the darkening clouds of the Depression, customers loved the insulated stoves—and not only Jewish customers.

Soon the company began adding stovetop ranges which were designed to accommodate a *blech* (Yiddish for sheet metal). The *blech* is used to cover stovetop burners on *Shabbos* as a precaution taken to avoid lighting a flame. Families found that if they heated the *blech* before *Shabbos*, it would retain that heat for many hours, allowing it to serve as something of a hotplate during the following day.

Soon, Welbilt began diversifying its product line by adding electric stoves and ranges, hoods, incinerators, and in later years, room air conditioners. In a letter to the company's dealers marking Welbilt's tenth anniversary, my uncle, A.P. heralded the company's phenomenal progress by announcing that the Welbilt Equi-Thermal Even Heat gas range has been designated "The World's Biggest Selling Popular Priced Range." He did not explain who did the designating. The company's 1939 product catalogue also promoted Welbilt's exhibit at the New York World's Fair where it would be unveiling "The Range of the Future."

During World War II and over the ensuing decades, Welbilt achieved growth primarily via acquisition of other manufacturers. Such companies as Cleveland Range and Frymaster soon fell under Welbilt ownership. Often an acquisition target was selected because of the quality of their engineering team. One practice that Henry initiated, that is being practiced to this day, is the retention of the brand name after a company has been absorbed into the Welbilt family. He wisely understood the value of good will and a good name.

"A good name is a valuable asset." he would say. "Why just throw it away?"

This is why, when Welbilt acquired the publicly-traded Michigan-Detroit Stove Company in 1955, it retained the Garland name that had been created a century before. It survives to this day as the Garland Group, a division that today makes commercial cooking equipment such as convection ovens, two-sided solid grills, and the newly developed induction ranges. In addition to the Garland brand, Welbilt gained ownership of a number of other well-known lines at the time such as: Jewel, Laurel, Wedgewood-Holly and A-B Stoves.

Michigan-Detroit Stove became a takeover target due to a series of faulty management decisions. In 1948, with sales reaching a peak of $21 million, the company went on an expansion program that grew its Detroit facility into a 23-building campus. They ventured into consumer electric ranges and auto parts. By 1953 Michigan-Detroit's bloated operations reported losses of $1.6 million on sales of only $9 million. Welbilt immediately began a plan to turn things around. Their first move was to sell off A-B Stoves, close the Detroit plant, and move it to Maspeth, Queens.

My father continued growing Welbilt through acquisition. In 1958, the company purchased a Lafayette, Indiana maker of home furnaces, Consolidated Industries. The following year it acquired the Wedgewood-Holly Corporation, a Culver City, California producer of high-end ranges. It was overseeing this company during the late sixties that led to my Las Vegas junkets described in Chapter Six. Welbilt entered the air conditioning market in 1960 via its purchase of American Coils Company. It was during this period of rapid growth that the misguided purchase of the Unagusta Furniture Company described in Chapter Four was carried out.

By this time Welbilt, which had also entered the home air conditioning market via its acquisition of American Coils Company, now had over 1000 employees and was producing 1000 stoves a day. It had become one of the leading stove manufacturers in the country, competing with the likes of General Electric, Westinghouse and Caloric.

By the end of 1960 Welbilt had plants in four states and Canada as well as the original Queens factory, where a new building was erected in 1964 for the manufacture of air-conditioning equipment as well as kitchen ranges. During the mid-1960's, I was primarily devoted to sales and product development. I had initiated the development of an innovative consumer-grade range hood that became a highly successful new product for us. It was at this juncture that I reached out to Larry Gross and asked him to join me at Welbilt. I was soon relying upon his considerable organizational and management skills, first as Personnel Director and later as my assistant. By now, the scope of my responsibilities had gradually grown to encompass the entire company.

Welbilt reached a new peak of $56.8 million in sales shortly before I fully took over operations, but by that time the company was already starting to bleed money. It operated in the red for the next five years—losing a total of $10.4 million—as Larry and I struggled to turn things around. In 1971, at the age of 29, I succeeded my father as president. As pointed out in Chapter Six, I became the youngest president of a publicly-traded Fortune 500 company, a record that stood through 1996 when it was broken by 27-year-old Michael Dell.

As we struggled to devise turnaround strategies, it became increasingly clear to me that the company could not survive by continuing to make and market consumer goods. As we began a program of planned divestiture and consolidation, we first turned to the five losing furniture companies that we owned. The biggest drain was Unagusta, which, after losing almost $6 million during 1971 and 1972, was sold for $5 million the following year. The Wedgewood-Holly stove division was sold in 1972.

A lamp manufacturing operation that Welbilt had formed was scrapped in 1974. The following year we decided to close down the original Queens plant and began actively pursuing the sourcing of domestic appliances in Canada, Italy, the far east and elsewhere in the U.S. We next transferred the production of our commercial cooking equipment to our newly-opened Freeland, Pennsylvania plant where we had relocated the manufacture of our oldest legacy line, Garland Stove. Later, we also manufactured a line of consumer microwave ovens at that plant.

Another major project was converting the original Welbilt buildings in Maspeth, Queens into a rental property in an effort to generate cashflow. The Maspeth campus had been built up in units over the years and we sort of unwound that process and broke it back down to the original spaces. Our rental tenants were mostly businesses in need of warehouse space—a market segment that was burgeoning at the time—as well as light industrial and small manufacturing concerns such as a corrugated box company and a soda soft drink maker. We really didn't care what they did there. As long as they were credit-worthy and were able to pay the rent, we took them in gladly.

As you may conclude from the foregoing, I had taken the reins at Welbilt at a very precarious time in its history. Yes, I did feel as though I had stepped into a quagmire. But, with Larry's support, I was able to bear the brunt of that period which I would describe as more or less living hand-to-mouth. We were forced to monitor our cash flow tightly to insure that this week's sales would cover next week's payroll. I would say that the two factors that enabled Welbilt to weather this stormy period were the accumulated good will and "good name" we had established with our lenders and vendors, as well as the wealth that our family had accumulated that was now being deployed to keep us afloat.

Looking back, I would have to say that this "trial by fire" during the early days of my leadership of Welbilt required the most effort and were the most arduous days of my entire business career.

By 1974 the word was out about our strapped financial conditions and we saw our stock fall as low as three cents a share. Stripped to the bone, we witnessed our sales drop to $15.8 million in 1975 and we were still losing money. Despite the cutbacks and divestitures, we still lost $2.4 million that year. With total assets of only $6 million and an average $2.2 million loss for the previous three fiscal years, we lost our listing on the New York Stock Exchange. This was the nadir of the Welbilt story as well as the key turning point.

I discovered that without SEC oversight I was able to exercise the type of bold governance that would make a real difference in our company's fortunes. As I explained to the editor of Appliance magazine for a 1989 cover story they later published about Welbilt:

"The really dynamic growth of the company began in the late 1970's when the restructuring was completed and a decision made to expand our commitment to food service equipment. We reviewed our goals and set new directions for the future. We had closed 12 divisions, retained Garland and shrunk the company to a solid and critical mass."

A New Era

I am pleased to say that the downsizing and consolidation salvage program was successful. It enabled Welbilt to return to financial health. After three straight profitable years it ended 1979 with net sales of $32.5 million and net income of $2.8 million. We resumed paying dividends in 1981 after a decade-long drought. Larry and I, with the assistance of Monte Shapiro, now began acquiring manufacturers of products that could be sold to fast-food chains. In 1982 we bought four food-service Sunbeam Corporation subsidiaries, including Frymaster, a company that had been providing equipment to Kentucky Fried Chicken and other large chain accounts since 1960. Also acquired at this point were Belshaw Brothers (a bakery equipment manufacturer) and Mile High, a producer of ice-making machines. Our engineers designed new equipment for these firms, with an emphasis on reducing labor costs. Frymaster, for example, began selling deep-fry equipment for chicken and french fries that automatically adjusted cooking time and temperatures, cleaned themselves, and shut themselves off. By 1989, largely due to other acquisitions, Belshaw systems were making about 65 percent of all the doughnuts in the world.

These measures led to some phenomenal growth. I am proud to say that Welbilt sales rose fourfold between 1982 and 1986. Between 1984 and 1988 Welbilt's compound annual earnings growth rate was 54 percent. During this period about 70 percent of our sales and slightly more of its profits were coming from commercial food-service equipment, including not only ranges, ovens, and appliances, but also kitchen ventilators, grease filters and extractors, and exhaust fans. The remainder came from domestic appliances, including the manufacture and sale of residential gas-fired furnaces, the sale of residential ranges, the sale and distribution of refrigerators, and the distribution of freezers and oil-filled unit heaters. In 1984, no longer in desperate need of positive cash flow, we sold off our Maspeth, Queens facility for $7.6 million and moved our executive offices to New Hyde Park, Long Island.

We ended 1987 with net income of $12.8 million on revenues of $234.3 million. Welbilt had grown to 16 subsidiaries, 11 factories (including plants in Canada and West Germany) and was now doing business in almost 100 countries. Our stock, once trading as low as 12 cents a share, was reinstated on the NASDAQ Stock Exchange and traded for as high as $28.25 in 1988. Revenues came to $273.6 million and earnings rose to a high of $6.2 million that year. This stellar performance, not surprisingly caught the attention of Wall Street speculators. Including a gentleman named Jerome Kohlberg, Jr. and his newly-minted private equity firm Kohlberg and Company.

CHAPTER NINE

THE WELBILT STORY PT. II

Cover story in the June, 1989 issue of industry trade publication, Appliance Magazine. (l-r) Richard L. Hirsch, president and CEO; David A. Hirsch, treasurer and CFO; Lawrence R. Gross, executive vice president.

"I will tell you the secret to getting rich on Wall Street. You try to be greedy when others are fearful. And you try to be fearful when others are greedy."

—Warren Buffett

The story of how Welbilt went private after being acquired for $265 million in a leveraged buyout led by Kohlberg & Company, is as intriguing as it is unlikely.

In 1988, Monte Shapiro, my trusted business mentor, began speaking to me about leveraged buy-outs (LBOs). An LBO refers to one company employing a significant amount of borrowed capital to acquire another company. The assets of the target company are used to secure the note. Monte informed me that Welbilt was being eyed by various parties as an attractive takeover candidate. He asked if I was willing to talk to someone about it. I said that I was.

The man he introduced me to was Jerome Kohlberg, Jr. an industry pioneer who, along with his son, James, had recently set up a new equity firm, Kohlberg & Company. Kohlberg had resigned from industry pioneer, Kohlberg Kravis Roberts (KKR) over differences in strategy. Kohlberg was opposed to the larger, often hostile LBOs of privately held companies like Beatrice Foods, RJR Nabisco and Safeway. Kohlberg wanted to return to his roots; to focus on acquiring companies that were facing operational or financial challenges in the middle-market space. And Welbilt fit this profile precisely. The idea was to acquire such companies with only moderate leverage and then concentrate on transactions that generated revenue growth and operational improvements while avoiding a crushing debt service.

Welbilt became Kohlberg & Co.'s first acquisition in 1988 as the company was taken private. The newly-configured company assumed a long-term debt of $187 million that was used to finance a large chunk of the deal. As part of the takeover, all outstanding shares of Welbilt, including those held by me, David, Monte and Larry were purchased by Kohlberg & Co. In addition to cash, we four were issued shares in the newly-configured company on a basis relative to our equity in the old company. Kohlberg & Co. retained a majority 60% ownership position.

I, along with my entire management team, including David, Larry Gross and Elizabeth Floyd, stayed on as salaried employees. Sadly, Monte Shapiro passed away not long afterwards.

I was able to continue my policies of divisional autonomy. I believed that the profit and loss centers are the responsibilities of the various divisional presidents. Monte supported me in this view. He commented to the industry press at the time: "We're interventionists only in terms of assistance and aid. We're hands off in terms of day-to-day operations." He was correct. We had developed a system whereby day-to-day operations were contained in a budget plan that then became the agreed-upon bible. These bibles determined how each division would work and how performance was measured.

Although I continued to serve as president after the takeover and although I was afforded the latitude to continue deploying my management methods, at the end of the day, I was unhappy. Instead of allowing me to focus on running Welbilt, Kohlberg insisted that I spend much of my time flying around the country with him looking at new acquisition targets. He would call me up and say "Meet me at the airport." I'd hop on his private jet and we'd head off to have a look at some midwest business that he had identified as a likely takeover candidate. Kohlberg would get in the backseat and fall asleep while I stayed up front fuming over the fact that I should have been back in my office managing Welbilt.

I was flattered that Kohlberg valued my opinion, but I wasn't really a money guy. I was an operations guy. I could see that Kohlberg was like the military general who thrives in battle but has no desire to govern when peace is achieved. Conquest is exciting. Running a day-to-day business can be drudgery. Likewise, Kohlberg knew exactly zero about stoves and furnaces. He had brought his own people in—all freshly-minted MBAs—who knew even less. They immediately began searching for ways for Welbilt to expand its operations.

The management philosophy that Larry and I had put into place over the years was to develop the product, develop the facilities, and particularly to develop the people who would lead the company to continued growth. We were always focused on improving our means and methods for today, for tomorrow and for the future. The new team that Kohlberg brought in were financial people and regarded our company not as an institution or as an engine of growth, but rather as an investment whose return needed to be maximized by all available means. At first, this meant further acquisition.

In April 1989, Welbilt acquired six divisions of Alco Standard Corp.'s Foodservice Equipment Group. These were Cleveland Range, a producer of steam-cooking equipment; Dean Industries, a manufacturer of gas and electric fryers and related equipment; Merco Products, a maker of food-warming equipment and broilers; Savory Equipment, a producer of countertop cooking appliances; U.S. Range, a manufacturer of commercial ranges, ovens, and broilers; and Alco World Trade, a marketer of food-service equipment.

Shortly after these acquisitions, Kohlberg placed a guy into top management, Marion H. Antonini, and asked me to work with him and train him. At the same time, it was clear that Kohlberg was grooming his son, James, to take over his operations at some point. It was rumored that James would soon be named as my successor as CEO of Welbilt. I could see the handwriting on the proverbial wall and started becoming sour on the whole deal. It was not a good marriage, to say the least. I finally approached Kohlberg and informed him that I wanted out as of a fixed date. He said that he would not stand in my way. It was, I believe, at this point, that Kohlberg and his crew changed direction. Instead of focusing on expansion, they began looking for ways to realize a quick return on their investment by selling off and unloading portions of the company. This was not something I wished to see happen. I was getting tired of the stress and I realized it was time for me to get out.

My formal exit from Welbilt management took place at the end of 1990. My team, consisting of Larry, Liz and others, agreed to stay on for a short time to facilitate the transition to the new Kohlberg & Co. management crew. My team departed at the end of the first quarter of 1991 but continued to provide verbal assistance to the new executive management team.

I walked away with an enormous sense of relief. The previous two years of working at cross-purposes with the new owners had been physically, as well as emotionally draining. I retained my ownership interest in Welbilt, which I would continue to hold through 1993.

I maintained a close relationship with Welbilt as I moved into the next phase of my career. Under my leadership and direct involvement, Welbilt's Appliance Industries division had continued to profit from its marketing of domestic appliances and housewares. During the 1980's, the division began marketing several consumer bread machines and continued operations after the LBO. According to industry sources, Appliance Industries commanded almost half of the consumer bread machine category by late 1991. The subsidiary also was sourcing and distributing other specialty kitchen appliances, compact refrigerators, and microwave ovens for the home, but only when the products dovetailed with the parent company's manufacturing and distribution of commercial food equipment. In the early 90's, Appliance Industries introduced a combination toaster, microwave and coffeemaker called the Breakfast Express. After experiencing substantial losses in this space, Welbilt finally decided to spin off the division

After my departure, the company headquarters were moved from New Hyde Park to Stamford, Connecticut. Welbilt suffered a loss of $13.8 million on sales of $357 million in 1991 but returned to modest profitability the following year and had net income of $6.6 million on sales of $426.5 million in 1993.

In November 1993, Welbilt went public again, offering common stock at $18 a share. Some of the proceeds were used to reduce the long-term debt, which stood at $126.2 million at the end of the year. It was at this point that our group (David, Larry and me) sold off our holdings in Welbilt and, as such, all my formal ties with the company that my family had founded came to an end—although I have kept in contact with the company's management over the ensuing decades.

Investors responded favorably to the offering, and in 1994 the stock rose as high as $33.50 a share. That year the company acquired Lincoln Foodservice Products, a manufacturer of ovens, commercial kitchen supplies, and other food-service equipment. In January 1995 Berisford International PLC, a British firm, acquired

Welbilt for $33.75 a share. The Kohlberg family held almost 47 percent of the stock at this time.

By 1996 Welbilt had evolved into a holding company for 12 subsidiaries or lines: Belshaw, Cleveland, Dean, Frymaster, Garland, Ice-O-Matic, Lincoln, Merco, Savory, U.S. Range, Varimixer, and Vent Master. The Garland Group consisted of units making Garland-brand, premium-line cooking equipment and distributing it worldwide. Frymaster was producing fryers and filtration systems and also overseeing Dean fryers and Varimixer mixing equipment. Lincoln, the world's largest manufacturer of commercial and institutional aluminum food-service utensils, also produced ovens, marketed kitchen cutlery, and imported and sold stainless-steel cookware with aluminum-clad bottoms. Belshaw was turning out 20 basic doughnut-making machines per day. Mile High was producing ice-makers under the Ice-O-Matic and Mile High brand names. Welbilt also maintained the engineering center in Tampa, Florida for developing new equipment.

Today, Welbilt, Inc. (WBT) stock has traded as high as $23 per share on the New York Stock Exchange. It is considered a small-cap company with a total capitalization of around $1 billion and $0.68 per share in earnings. It boasts 5100 full-time employees and its management team has been headed since November of 2018 by CEO, William C. Johnson. Cindy Egnotovich sits as the chair of the company's board of directors. Prior to taking over as CEO of Welbilt, Johnson had served in the same capacity for Chart Industries, Inc., a global manufacturer of highly engineered equipment for the industrial gas, energy, and biomedical industries.

I am proud that the company my family founded in the 1920's has endured and flourished for nearly a century. At the same time, I am equally proud of the record of accomplishment achieved during the next phase of my business career as my brother David, Larry Gross, and Elizabeth Floyd established the Concurrent Industries Group.

CHAPTER TEN

PEOPLE, PRODUCT, FINANCE

"Know what you own, and know why you own it."
—Peter Lynch

I have always believed that a good motto or slogan can help people focus on what's really important. For example, my mentor, Monte Shapiro, was a wizard when it came to delegating responsibility, both when he ran General Instrument and after he joined me at Welbilt. His oft-repeated motto was "You organize, you deputize, and then you supervise." Essentially this meant that as a business leader, you should avoid the temptation to micromanage the people working under you. Agree on a plan, find the best people to carry it out and then give them the space to execute. Finally, supervise by fairly evaluating the outcomes they produce.

The motto that serves as the title of this chapter contains the watchwords that I inherited from my father. Words that became my guiding strategy during my active years as a business leader. Job number one, I always felt, was to identify and attract the right people to my team. People who not only demonstrated a strong work ethic, but also those who shared my vision and sense of direction. Second was deciding on the right product that would be welcomed and then embraced by our customers. The final step was to determine how to produce and distribute that product on a cost-efficient basis so that it would produce value for our shareholders.

Of the three watchwords, the first, People, is clearly the most critical. That is why I worked tirelessly, during my years at Welbilt, to recruit and incentivize our managers and workforce. A basic component of this strategy for which I take credit was the establishment of separate leadership groups at each of our subsidiaries. Each division had its own team of top level executives who enjoyed a high degree of autonomy and authority. They were, for example, free to design their own employee bonus and benefit programs. As long as a division was hitting our projected performance targets, we, in the head office, did not interfere.

I was quoted in the trade press shortly after the LBO that you'll read about later, as saying: "In a nutshell, people and planning make up our competitive edge. We have been able to attract, develop, and retain some of the best people in the industry—and some from outside the industry. I think our divisional management incentives are key strengths responsible for our competitive advantage." *(Appliance Magazine; June, 1989)*

This management style produced stunning results. By giving each subsidiary such latitude, we succeeded in giving the leadership team a sense of proprietary interest. They became fully invested, not only on a professional level, but also on a personal and even emotional level with the fortunes of their division. My frustration at not being able to continue operating in this way after the Kohlberg LBO was a factor that led to my decision to move on. Of course, my departure led to the inevitable question of "What next?" I wasn't sure, but as I surveyed the industry landscape of the early 1990's I was certain of one thing. Whatever new venture I would become involved with, I would only do so if I could operate under these watchwords that had successfully guided my career for more than twenty years.

It took about a year, but I, along with Larry Gross, Liz Floyd and my brother, David, set up a financial holding company, based out of our office at 375 Park Avenue, New York, whose initial mission was to acquire and manage companies in the commercial and consumer kitchen equipment space. In casting about for a name, I again turned to my late mentor and friend, Monte Shapiro, for inspiration. Monte always used to say that he liked people who were concurrent rather than consecutive (see Chapter Seven). People who could tackle several tasks simultaneously and not one after another. I shared this outlook and decided on the name Concurrent Industries Group, L.L.C. or C.I.G. as the moniker for our new entity.

C.I.G. can rightly be dubbed a family investment office or private holding company. Our investments are primarily confined to public and private equity, structured debt, and real estate. While we initially focused on the foodservice industry, we have since broadened our horizon to include the fitness industry and light manufacturing. This expansion of our scope was accelerated once my son, Adam, joined me at C.I.G. While what we do may fall under the rubric of venture capital—both early and late-stage financing—we continue to adhere to my philosophy of investing in people, not just ideas.

Our first acquisition was a food equipment OEM (original equipment manufacturer) based in Peachtree City, Georgia called Franklin Industries. They produced a line of commercial kitchen equipment, Franklin Chef, that included fryers, broilers, ovens, etc. While I eventually did buy a home in Atlanta, we operated the business out of our New York office. Eventually I brought a gentleman by the name of Harvey Lieberman into the Franklin operation. Harvey operated a housewares factory in Brooklyn and we merged that line into those being produced by Franklin. I was also successful in attracting a few of the talented engineers with whom I had worked at Welbilt into the Franklin operation.

This move did not, as you might expect, violate any non-compete agreements I had agreed to prior to leaving Welbilt. The reason was that Franklin's domestic products were mainly focused on the housewares industry—their primary distribution partner was Home Depot—whereas Welbilt operated in the appliance space. Also the engineers in question were of retirement age and, as such, were excluded from any restrictions about my hiring Welbilt employees.

As mentioned, Larry Gross and Liz Floyd stayed on at Welbilt for a short time after my departure and then joined me when I set up C.I.G. Based on my dedication to always finding the right people for my team, I considered myself very fortunate to be working with both Larry and Liz. Elizabeth Floyd had served as my right-hand assistant during many of my years at Welbilt. I had come to trust her abilities and dedication, and therefore gave her wide authority in our operations at C.I.G. Liz was a University of Chicago graduate and extremely bright. She not only handled all my correspondence but was also a great sounding board for both me and Larry. Sadly, Elizabeth Floyd passed away on March 15, 2015.

My son Adam joined C.I.G. after leaving his previous positions at American Express and two national health club chains. He is a tremendous asset and currently manages my entire family office, with holdings in public/private equity, real estate, and venture capital. While David and I have more or less retired from day to day activities, Adam remains active and continues to successfully and concurrently manage the companies in our group.

Concluding the active business phase of my life has permitted me the time to focus increasingly on my philanthropic pursuits. In recent years I have been guided by a quote that is attributed to one of my major heroes, Winston Churchill:

"We make a living by what we get, but we make a life by what we give."

This notion encapsulates the essence of philanthropy for me. As discussed, my parents were uniquely devoted to causes benefiting the Jewish community and I am proud to say that I have tried to sustain and expand that legacy during my own lifetime. I discuss some of my philanthropic activities in Chapter Thirteen.

Richard L. Hirsch

Photo Album
Part II

Making a "business deal" in China.

Greeting students at school in Tel Aviv.

June 22, 1998. At a Be'er HaGolah Gala Dinner at the New York Hilton. (l-r) Leonard Kestenbaum, me, Ira Rennert, Chief Rabbi of Israel Meir Lau, Matt Maryles, Jason Curry.

With my new wife, Elaine Bedell, at our wedding on February 14, 2002.

François Houpert, my good friend and associate from France.

Giving advice to, or taking advice from, Israeli President, Shimon Peres.

(l-r) Israeli Minister of Finance, Yuval Steinitz; President Reuven Rivlin; Israel Bonds President, Joshua Matza; Israel Bonds Vice President, Richard Hirsch (me)

Armand and Jeannie Lindenbaum visiting us in Palm Beach.

*At the bris of my first-born grandchild at the Fifth Avenue Synagogue.
(l-r) Cantor Joseph Malovany; me holding baby Ryan Hirsch; my son, Daniel Hirsch.*

Cousin Ed and Judy Prager in Montreal.

With former British Prime Minister, Tony Blair.

With Rick Caron, executive vice president at Welbilt headquarters in Florida.

*(l-r) Back row: Daniel and Carolyn Hirsch holding Victoria; David Hirsch; me; Joyce; A
Jessica; Patrick (Coyle); Stephanie; Jason Hirsch; Rochelle Hirsch.
(r-l) Front row. Elaine (kneeling); Matthew, William, and Ryan Hirsch.*

(l-r) Izzy Tapoohi; Jaime Schmidt, Israeli Prime Minister, Benjamin Netanyahu; and me.

Sharing the podium with Israeli Prime Minister, Benjamin Netanyahu.

Richard L. Hirsch

With author and reporter, Bob Woodward (circled) at an Israel Bond Young Leadership Conference in Washington, D.C.
I am seeted in the center, 5th from right, next to Izzy Tapoohi.

With Warren Buffett.

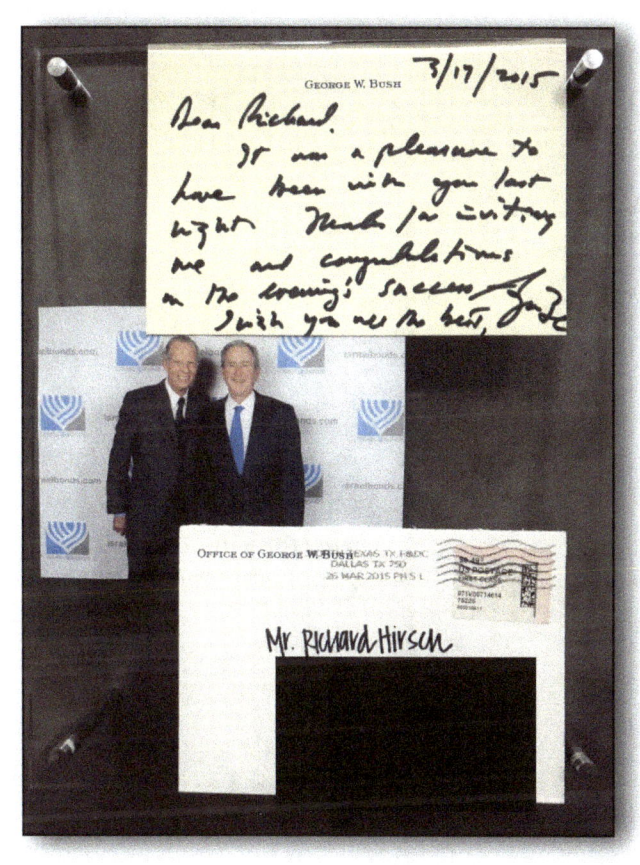

Note and photo from former president, George W. Bush.

Our good friends, Robert and and Lise Issenman in Montreal, Canada.

*(l-r) Me holding grand-
daughter, Millie;
My son, Adam, holding
granddaughter, Lucie.*

*Teaching grandpa
how to play.
With granddaughter,
Victoria Hirsch*

Sharing a joke with grandson, Cedar Hirsch Sweeney.

My grandchildren, Cedar and Lola Sweeney at home.

Back row: Armand and Jeannie Lindenbaum; Elaine and me.
Seated: Gail Propp, John Steindecker, Larry Friedland, Rebecca Steindecker.

With Ric Smith in Palm Beach.

Two of my grandchildren. Big sister Lucie Hirsch with baby Millie.

(l-r) Grandchildren William, Ryan, Matthew and Victoria Hirsch.

Attending a Jewish Student Union-sponsored Holocaust Memorial Event at Spanish River High School in Boynton Beach, Florida.

At Spanish River High School in Boynton Beach, FL with the JSU. (l-r) Todd Cohn, Mal Dorman, Edith Greenfield, Danny Abraham, Richard Duval, me, and Benjamin Gonsher.

Our friends, Bonnie and Steve Stern, in their lovely Palm Beach home.

My brother-in-law, Mickey Friedman and my sister, Carole Friedman in New York City.

Richard L. Hirsch

Chapter Eleven
Family Matters

Always forward.
Two of my grandchildren in Napa Valley. Summer, 2019.

"Happiness is having a large, loving, caring, close-knit family...in another city."

— George Burns

As discussed in Chapter One, my family life changed dramatically after the loss of our son, Larry, in 1972. Little by little, Joyce and I began growing steadily apart. Whether this was due to our belief in the inevitability of this outcome is hard to say. I do feel that this listing away from each other was not due primarily to guilt, although there was some of that. I never blamed Joyce for improper care of Larry. I know that she always acted in our son's best interests and did everything she could possibly have done to avoid what happened. Likewise, she did not blame me for being away from home at the time of the crisis. She knew that I was working very hard to rescue the company our family had founded and that my work required a good deal of travel. After Larry's death I found I was spending less and less time at home, while at the same time, Joyce had taken up activities that did not involve me. She pursued her golf and bridge foursomes with a passion. Joyce was doing her thing and I was doing mine. We both became very intent in moving on with our lives.

After several years of this ever-growing "marital distancing," we both realized the hard fact that, for all practical purposes, our marriage was over. Yet, for that classic reason: "the sake of the kids," we did not consider divorce until more than ten years after Larry's death. Throughout this period, Joyce was incredibly devoted to the welfare of our children. She became a true "super-Mom," and remains one to this day. By the early 1980's we both recognized that, while still living under one roof, we had been emotionally separated for some time. There were no third parties involved in our eventual decision to divorce. It was simply that after so many years of virtual estrangement, we both agreed that it was time to call it quits.

Once the decision had been reached, our next concern was how to inform our kids. I was a wreck trying to figure out how to tell them of our decision without making them feel as if they were in any way to blame. We decided to sit down with them to inform them of our decision, and were very relieved afterward because each one, Daniel, Michelle and Adam, said they understood our reasons for divorcing and agreed that it would be for the best. In fact, they all commented that they were surprised that it took us this long to reach this point. I know that it's never easy for children—even older ones—when faced with their parents' divorce, but I believe to this day that by informing them openly and honestly, we handled things the right way. We promised each of them that despite the divorce, their parents would remain friends and in full contact. We have kept that promise to this day and Joyce and I remain on excellent terms.

As part of the settlement, Joyce took possession of the house in Atlantic Beach and our Manhattan apartment, but these days she spends most of her time at her home in Boca West. Although she chose not to remarry, she has enjoyed two long-term relationships and has fashioned a wonderful life for herself.

Once we had made the decision to divorce and how to work out the logistics that would cause the least disruption to the family, I found myself in need of lodgings. I started searching for a bachelor apartment in Manhattan and, through a good friend at the time, I contacted a real estate agent who turned out to be a godsend in more ways than one.

Elaine Bedell knows how to make a great first impression, both professionally and personally. Tall and slender, she possessed an engaging charm that I immediately found attractive. I only half-jokingly believe that if she had not come along when she did, I would never have found a place to stay and would still be living with Joyce.

At our first meeting Elaine came prepared with two realistic possibilities to consider. Apparently, at the time, short term rentals were rare, so she had to think outside of the box for a solution. While both options were excellent, I preferred the second, which was an apartment that had been on the market for sale. Elaine was able to negotiate with the owner to agree to rent it to me for a few months. As a result, I was able to sign a three month lease (with an option for another term) in a beautiful penthouse apartment with a gorgeous terrace in a great neighborhood.

After viewing this apartment, Elaine and I were sitting in my car, still parked at the curb, discussing the details of wrapping up the deal when I received a call on my "shoebox-sized" car phone—still something of a novelty at the time. At this point Elaine excused herself, got out of the car and stood waiting by the curb. I rolled down the window and asked:

"What are you doing? Why did you get out?"

"To give you some privacy," she replied without missing a beat. That gesture impressed on me that I was dealing with someone who was not only courteous, but able to intelligently assess new situations. My estimation of Elaine's capabilities turned out to be accurate. Not only did she deftly negotiate the deal, she made the moving in friction-free and actually very pleasant. Sensing my cluelessness about setting up a household, she took it upon herself to make sure everything I needed was there when I moved in. This included two sets of dishes, pots and pans and cutlery that I would need for a Kosher kitchen. She provided my new sheets and towels, and even located a house-keeper to make my life worry free.

Although I did have a group of ladies I would run with in Central Park in the mornings during this time, I really was too busy for much social interaction. I recall receiving phone calls from friends asking me to meet single ladies they thought I might like to get to know, but I wasn't too interested. Besides, I was getting to know Elaine, who was becoming a valuable, trusted friend. I soon discovered that I could depend on her for just about everything and the more I got to know her, the more I liked her. I never slipped into the role of "swinging bachelor," although I certainly had every opportunity to do so.

About a year after meeting Elaine, our close friendship moved into the next phase, as our meetings happily and easily turned into dates. Elaine was an avid horse-woman, so in order to keep up I started accompanying her on her weekend rides. I wasn't really a rider, but over the years, I had taken many "first" lessons, so at least I knew which end of the horse to put the carrots in. Elaine found a horse that was perfect for both my personality and level of experience. He was a well-schooled Appaloosa, a beautiful breed, originally bred by the Nez Perce Indians and easily recognized by their roan coats and white rumps. Since I am allergic to most animals, hay, pollen, flowers and just about everything Elaine can't live without, I would have to ride with every bit of skin covered (this get-up was dubbed my Hazmat outfit). Elaine would then bring me the horse well upwind of the barn, and I would need to take a Benadryl in order to survive the ride. My horse was originally named White Feather, but in recognition of the required medication, we ended up calling him Benny.

Benny and I turned out to be perfect together. He was patient, trustworthy and so smart that he knew to look both ways when crossing roads. He could balance me perfectly, and was relaxed enough to stay in the back of the pack where we could both enjoy nature and think our private thoughts. After Benny, I started riding another prince of a horse named Sunny, who really made me look good. It was one of the happiest times of my life, riding with the many friends we had made over some of the most beautiful countryside—all just 50 miles north of New York City. As Ronald Reagan used to say, "Nothing is as good for the inside of a man as the outside of a horse."

Our riding activities led to our buying a beautiful home in the town of North Salem, New York. It was only an hour's drive from the city, so we spent every weekend there as an escape from the rigorous work schedules we both were maintaining. The house was set on 15 idyllic acres and included a huge pond, a barn with a corral, flowing meadows, woodlands and magnificent rock outcroppings. I had been brought up in the city and was urban through and through (and, I like to think, urbane as well), so initially I was much like Woody Allen, who claimed he was at "two" with nature. Elaine, by contrast, was never happier than when she was in the garden, digging, planting and pruning, all the while surrounded by animals.

Thanks to Elaine, I eventually grew to love the sheer natural beauty of the place, the peacefulness of observing the bird and animal life, and the glorious changing of the seasons. We shared many weekends in North Salem with our family and friends. I vividly remember one long winter's weekend when my daughter, Michelle, visited from California, bringing along her new dog, Muna, a fantastic chocolate lab who had never seen snow. Each day we went outside exploring the pond and meadows, going on long walks through the woods behind the house while Muna ran back and forth playing in the snow, having the best time of her doggie life. When the weekend was over and we were packing the car for our trip home, Muna refused to get in the car. She ran back to the door and planted herself firmly on the threshold, clinging to it with all her might, and howling her sadness at leaving the place. It was both hilarious and heartbreaking, and the experience provided us with an even greater appreciation of our good fortune to be living in that fabulous place.

Although we enjoyed riding around the backwoods, both Elaine and I had also been around the block a few times. We had been in marriages that ended in divorce, a fact that made us both leery of jumping into a new marriage. Elaine's first husband had run off with his secretary, and while my experience was not nearly as emotionally scarring, neither of us wanted to rush into anything and possibly risk hurting the terrific relationship we had been building.

My divorce was legally concluded in 1998 and I was free to marry should we choose to do so. Of all of Elaine's endearing qualities, her superior intellect is the one I found the most attractive. I finally came to the wise conclusion that it would be a good idea to be married to someone smarter that I am, and the fact that she agreed only proves how smart she is.

Once again, there was no formal down-on-one-knee proposal. No "Ah-ha!" moment when our outlooks changed direction and we decided to wed. Elaine and I had been talking about getting married for a while and everyone just assumed that we would do so at some point. We more-or-less just slid into it. I recall discussing marriage with Elaine during one of our scenic hikes through the Bordeaux wine country in the South of France. It was in the early summer of 2001 and we had been discussing making wedding plans in a few months time. But then, the romantic mood was broken as my cell phone rang. This surprised us both since, in those days, it was difficult getting a decent cellular signal in midtown Manhattan—much less in a rural vineyard of the French wine country. It was my son, Daniel, who shared the good news that he had gotten engaged and that he and Carolyn were planning to marry in October. We did not wish to detract from their spotlight so we pushed our own wedding plans into the following year. In the interim, Elaine's mother became gravely ill and Elaine expressed her desire for us to marry before her mother passed away. I asked her to name the date.

I had warned Elaine that I would never remember our anniversary, so she wisely chose Valentine's Day as our wedding day, playing the odds that I would at least have a chance at remembering that date. Good choice, as I have never forgotten our romantic anniversary over all these years, and we always try to do something special with our friends to help commemorate the day.

Our wedding was a tasteful and understated affair, graciously held in the inviting and elegant home of my brother and sister-in-law, David and Rochelle. David served as my best man while Rabbi Rachman officiated. Happily, it was attended by all our closest friends, but sadly, Elaine's mother was too ill to be there. She was told about it and shown photos soon after, and was delighted to know we had finally married. She died a month later. Elaine and I had waited years before tying the knot and I am happy to report that it remains tightly tied to this day.

The question of our religious identities had pretty much been resolved by the time we got married. I had explained to Elaine about my strict observance of Jewish practices including the *Kashruth* dietary laws. While this part of my life was at first alien to her, to her everlasting credit, she made it her business to educate herself so she could facilitate all aspects of my *"Shomer Shabbos"* level of observance. Years before we got married, Elaine had presented me with a most unusual birthday present. I learned of it by reading her words in a birthday card:

> Dearest Richard. In searching for yet another perfect birthday present, I found something I think will be more meaningful than one more bathrobe or cigar humidor. I have spoken to Rabbi Rackman and he has agreed to counsel me for my conversion to Judaism. I am hoping this will bring us closer as a couple as I know how much your faith means to you. Just one warning: I was a pretty lousy Catholic, and

I'm not sure I'll make a very good Jew, but I promise I'll give it my best. All my love and Happy Birthday!

Loosely raised as a Catholic, Elaine prepared for an *Halachic* (legal) conversion under the esteemed authority of Rabbi (Menachem) Emanuel Rackman. Rabbi Rackman had taken over the pulpit at the Fifth Avenue Synagogue in 1967, succeeding Rabbi Immanuel Jakobovits who had been elected to serve as the Chief Rabbi of the United Hebrew Congregations of the Commonwealth in the U. K. Rackman had served as the president of the Rabbinical Council of America and he had also served as the president of Bar-Ilan University in the 1970's and 1980's. But perhaps his most noteworthy accomplishments arose from his campaign to draw attention to the plight of Refuseniks in the Soviet Union. These were Jews who had been imprisoned, or otherwise punished, for openly demanding that the Soviet regime allow them to immigrate to Israel.

Having Rabbi Rackman conduct Elaine's conversion was particularly apt since his previous career as a lawyer was focused on expanding the role and rights of women in Orthodox Jewish life. Not surprisingly, his advocacy for women's rights made him something of an anathema in certain more conservative quarters of the Orthodox community. He was particularly assiduous in resolving the dilemma of the *Agunah*. An *Agunah*, under Jewish law, is a woman who is unable to remarry because her husband would not grant her a *Gett* (a bill of divorcement). He spoke of this work with Elaine during her studies and I recall how impressed Rabbi Rackman was with Elaine's depth of knowledge about Jewish law and ritual. This fact was borne out when it came time for Elaine to undergo a ritual bath in the *Mikvah* as part of the conversion process. Jewish tradition prescribes that a candidate for conversion undergo a profound symbol of radical change. This is called *tevilah* and it is the *sine qua non* and the core component of conversion into Judaism. It is from this tradition that the Christian practice of baptism and becoming "born again" emerged.

Elaine underwent the ceremonial bath on a frigid January New York morning. She was asked to take off all clothing, jewelry, and make-up, and let her hair hang freely. The matron then checked her for any tattoos or piercings, strictly forbidden in the Jewish tradition. After her first total submersion, she was asked to recite a blessing and then underwent two more total submersions into the chilly water, each followed by the blessing. She shared with me what happened next:

"I was shivering with cold as the matron handed me a thin robe to put on. I was then escorted, barefoot and dripping, into a cold adjoining room where I was told to sit down on a rickety metal folding chair next to a fully clothed, warmly dressed Rabbi Rackman. Our chairs were facing a tribunal of rabbis I had never met before."

This was the *Beth Din*. A *Beth Din*, or "house of judgement," is an Orthodox rabbinic court composed of three learned Rabbis. It is invested with legal powers in matters related to Jewish religious observance.

As Elaine recounted to me later, the three rabbis began peppering her with questions to test her knowledge of Jewish law and ritual. "It was like taking the orals for a doctorate degree," she observed. As she sat there shivering in the unheated room and slowly turning blue, she managed to respond correctly to each question, leaving the rabbis impressed with her training and preparation.

Finally, having run out of questions for her, the chief rabbi concluded with, "Do you have any questions for us?" "No," is the typical response, but Elaine is anything but typical.

"As a matter of fact I do," she responded. They urged her to proceed.

"On the last day of Sukkoth, I watch Richard beating the ground repeatedly with a bundle of branches and leaves," she said. "What is the meaning of this ritual?"

The rabbis were taken aback that a candidate for conversion would even consider a question of such Talmudic depth. They unanimously ruled that Elaine, having asked such a profound question, had the right qualities to undergo a *giyur* (conversion) and was indeed well-prepared to become a member of the community of Israel. Each rabbi then proceeded to give her a different answer to the question, thereby proving the old saw, "Two Jews, three opinions".

The chief rabbi again asked, "Any further questions?"

"Yes", she said through chattering teeth. "Am I Jewish yet?"

This brought about a laugh and a sudden realization of how cold she must have been sitting wet in a freezing room. She was excused.

Briefly, the ritual that Elaine was asking about takes place on the seventh day of the holiday, *Sukkot* (The Feast of Tabernacles). The day is called *Hoshana Rabbah*, or the day of many Hosannas (shouts of praise and supplication). It is the day the divine judgements issued on Yom Kippur are finalized. It's also known as the Day of the Willow because the primary observance—one that emulates a ritual practiced on this day in the ancient Temple—is the taking of a bundle of five willow branches and striking the ground five times with them. Each stroke is intended to temper each of the five levels of divine harshness and bring about a merciful outcome for the people of Israel.

Elaine was loosely brought up as a Catholic, but by the time she was in her teens, she had lost her trust in the Church. Her mother had practiced "Catholicism Lite," attending church on major holidays, and her father, deceased by the time we met, was a non-practicing Jew. His only remaining connection to his religion had been his eating habits, which were mostly Kosher, making it easier for Elaine to adapt to our entirely Kosher home.

Today Elaine could be called a "Practicing Jew," as distinguished from an "Observant Jew." An Observant Jew is one who attempts to fulfill all the practices, restrictions, and constraints that are among the 613 commandments found in the Torah, while a Practicing Jew is one who observes the rituals found to be personally meaningful. Elaine keeps a Kosher home because she knows it's important to me. Although I regularly attend synagogue, she does not, although she will accompany me on special occasions. Is she a good Jew? Absolutely, because every Friday night, wherever we may be, she lights the *Shabbos* candles and there are challah and wine on the table. As for myself, am I a Practicing Jew or an Observant Jew? Actually, I fall squarely into the category of a Neurotic Jew. That is, I observe many of the Jewish practices, yet feel inadequate because I cannot bring myself to fulfill them all. As my mother, in true Yiddishe Mama fashion, would tell me: "It doesn't matter what you do, Richard, as long as you feel guilty about it."

After we moved our primary residency to Florida, Elaine retired fully from her real estate career and now concentrates on her personal interests. Happily, I am one of them, as she is fully devoted to my care and feeding. She's known for the beautiful breakfasts I enjoy every morning. Often our morning guests insist on taking photos and have urged me to send them to food magazines to grace their covers. She is not only an accomplished artist, she's a skilled writer and has played a major role in the production of this book.

Our families meshed together very well, growing closer over the years. While Elaine is highly supportive of my many philanthropic activities, she is not directly involved with them on a day-to-day basis. Finally, let me point out what a wonderful relationship Elaine enjoys with my three adult children: Daniel, Michelle, and Adam. Here's a little update on each of them.

Daniel attended Boston University after which he went to work briefly in the fashion industry, and then for the Canadian aviation company, Bombardier. He finally settled into the food equipment service business, drawn to the creation and design of new product lines. Today Daniel operates a New Jersey ice machine servicing company, FixIce, that also handles soft-serve ice cream equipment. Daniel is married to Carolyn, the daughter of a well-known Montreal composer and opera singer, Judith Cohen Lechter, who recently performed her Oratorio for World Peace at the Vatican. Daniel and Carolyn have provided us with four wonderful grandchildren.

My daughter, Michelle, graduated from the University of Michigan where she studied at the School of Kinesiology. Michelle excelled as a student and at a certain point during college she became very interested in natural foods and organic agriculture. She operated an organic farm in Michigan and did the same after moving to Berkeley. In California, Michelle obtained her kinesiologist license and founded a chain of acupuncture and herbalist centers (Octagon Community Acupuncture Clinics) in North Oakland as well as a highly successful Natural Health website (BeyondTheMountainWellness.com). In 2013 Michelle married Arron Sweeney, a former sommelier and Napa Valley wine expert. Arron has had a successful career in real estate, and today enjoys working as a wine consultant for some of the area's finest restaurants. The couple are the parents of two more of my wonderful grandchildren.

Adam also attended the University of Michigan where he, like Michelle, studied kinesiology. After graduation, Adam went to work for Crunch Fitness Centers, where he helped the chain to expand from ten to 27 locations in three years. From there, he joined another fitness company, David Barton Gym, where he met his future wife, Jessica Sylvester. Upon leaving David Barton, Adam joined American Express during which time he earned his M.B.A. from the Deming Scholars Program at the Fordham University Graduate School of Business. Adam later joined Larry Gross and me in expanding our family's investment office, Concurrent Industries Group, or C.I.G., which he currently manages and runs (see Chapter Ten). Adam and Jess have also given us two wonderful grandchildren.

Because of Adam's involvement with the School of Kinesiology at Michigan, I came into contact with the school's Director of the Office of Student Services, Shelly Kovacs, who encouraged me to help her set up funding projects on behalf of the school. In 2010, Shelly's devotion to the school was recognized via the establishment of a special scholarship fund in her name.

"The most amazing thing about the scholarship is that most people don't have the opportunity for recognition and appreciation in their lifetime," she said at the time. "Most people have to retire or die in order to receive such a special honor."

My Super Siblings

My older sister, Carole, was born in 1938, the year of the Munich Pact and the Joe Louis-Max Schmeling fight. Carole, by all accounts, is the most like my mother, Myrtle, in terms of her devotion to Jewish causes and philanthropy. By the same token, she is in many ways like my father, Henry, in her penchant for working humbly and quietly behind the scenes. She is known for her sharp mind and her unflagging energy.

As a young woman Carole studied art at what was then the Carnegie Institute of Technology and then obtained her degree at NYU. Carole continued her artistic endeavors into her forties and became well known as a gifted sculptor and painter.

On December 22, 1958, Carole was married to Yale graduate, Michael L. (Mickey) Friedman in the very first function ever to be held at the newly-opened Fifth Avenue Synagogue. She has been a stalwart pillar of support for that institution ever since. Mickey worked with the Hirsch family and Monte Shapiro for a bit at Micamold (which later became General Instrument). At about the same time that I started working with David at Welbilt (the early 1980's), Mickey founded a brokerage firm called First New York Securities that grew, over the next thirty years, into one of Wall Streets' preeminent trading partnerships.

Mickey also became involved at Fifth Avenue Synagogue as the director of its two-year pre-school program. He did that through the early 70's after which it folded and was revived in the 90's by my sister-in-law, Rochelle, David's wife, who took over and has run the preschool ever since.

In the early 1960's, Mickey and Carole became the parents of three children: Debbie, Lisa, and Jonny. My nephew, Jonny, today is a successful agent-broker and vice-president at the Sterling & Sterling agency in Woodbury, New York. He is also the founder of Micamold Management, operator of a multi-manager, multi-strategy hedge fund named after the enamel capacitor company where his father Mickey got his start. Jonny works at Micamold Management with two of his cousins, David and Rochelle's sons, Jason and Jeffrey Hirsch.

Carole has proudly and dilligently carried on the the legacy of my mother's philanthropic work. She has devoted her life to tireless support for the numerous causes my parents believed in. In particular Yeshiva Torah Vodaath, the Fifth Avenue Synagogue, and the UJA.

Like my brother David, Carole and Mickey, both in their eighties, remain avid lifetime golfers and may frequently be found on the links at their Rancho Santa Fe home near San Diego. Their family has grown to include four grandchildren, three great-grandchildren, and, as of this writing, another great-grandchild is due shortly.

My younger brother, David, graduated from the Ramaz School in Manhattan's Upper East Side and went on to study at Cornell University where he majored in engineering, graduating in 1965. He obtained his MBA at Columbia and then joined the family real estate company, Padar. At Padar he worked with my uncle, A.P. and was involved in the development of primarily residential real estate in the tri-state area.

David met his future wife, Rochelle, a Queens College graduate with an M.A. from N.Y.U., in 1969 at Grossinger's Resort in the Catskills. Both were there celebrating Passover with their families. The resort proved to be the great matchmaker of its day and David and Rochelle were yet another of their success stories. They became a serious couple, adding one more marriage to Grossinger's' impressive record. They wed in 1971, have three children, and now have two grandchildren as well.

After Padar was sold in the early 1980's, David joined me at Welbilt. We worked together until the company was sold via a leveraged buy-out in 1988. At that point, David joined me when I put together C.I.G. and acquired Franklin Industries in Atlanta. But throughout those years, David pursued a concurrent career as a commodity trading advisor, specializing in precious metal futures.

Although he is retired today, David still trades commodity contracts, but just for the family.

Like our sister, David has devoted himself to supporting the various philanthropic passions pursued by our mother, Myrtle. Chief among these are the Fifth Avenue Synagogue and the Israeli Philharmonic Orchestra. David only recently stepped down as the orchestra's president in 2019. He enjoys playing the piano and his role with the Philharmonic coincides with David's deep love of music.

Along with being a life-long supporter of Yeshvia Torah Vodaath, David and Rochelle were instrumental in founding the Be'er Hagolah Institutes, a pre-K through 12 Brooklyn day school that accepts all students regardless of financial ability. David and Rochelle were particularly involved in the school's program of assisting Russian Jewish families as they resettled in New York after the fall of the Soviet Union.

David and Rochelle were also founders of a New York branch of Hatzalah, a volunteer EMS (emergency medical service) organization. Hatzalah means "rescue" in Hebrew and the group provides 24/7 no-cost emergency transportation and other services primarily to New York's Jewish community. Hatzalah is credited with saving many lives during the 2020 Coronavirus pandemic.

David has also been deeply involved in our family's long-standing support of Miftan Alon—part of the UJA's Project Renewal. The couple is likewise devoted to a host of other worthwhile causes such as the Teen Philanthropy Program, the Healthcare Chaplaincy, the Schneider School, and the Open University of Israel, one of the world's first online colleges.

In the early 1980's, David and Rochelle were searching for a place to begin the Jewish education of their two-year-old daughter, Stefanie. The pre-school at the Fifth Avenue Synagogue that had been run by David's brother-in-law, Mickey Friedman, had been closed for more than a decade and few other attractive options existed. Rochelle recognized the need and spent the next two years setting up the synagogue's Creative Play School for children aged

2 and 3. Rochelle served as the school's director for many years and today heads its Board of Directors. It offers a child-centered creative curriculum that includes music, movement, art and yoga. Children are taught about Jewish holidays and traditions in a warm and nurturing environment.

David and Rochelle's son, Jason, as well as their daughter, Stefanie, both graduated from Cornell University. Jason, like his dad, went on to obtain his MBA at NYU. Stefanie traveled to England after graduation and took her master's degree in curatorial studies at the Goldsmith School of the University of London. Today she works as a curator for a company called Indiwalls.

As mentioned, both of David and Rochelle's sons, Jason and Jeffrey, work with their cousin, Jonny Friedman at Micamold Management. In addition, Jeffrey operates a highly popular website called New York Social Diary, founded by a colorful personage named David Patrick Columbia. Jeffrey served as David's intern and now is his partner in producing this extremely popular online journal that serves as a social, historical and cultural chronicle of life in New York City.

There's no question as to whether my family ties helped to shape the course of my life over the years. Both in the realms of business and philanthropy, I always have looked to my family for support and for guidance. All in all, I hope that it's obvious from this brief summary how much I cherish these relationships and how much pride I derive from being a member of such an outstanding family.

Chapter Twelve
With A Little Help From My Friends

Running in Central Park with Danny Baldinger.

"A real friend is one who walks in when the rest of the world walks out."

— Walter Winchell

If I wrote down the many things in my life for which I am thankful, at the top of the page would be that I've been extremely lucky to have made so many great friends over the course of my life. I'll try to list these cherished people in chronological order, since in order of importance, they are all equal. I apologize if I have unwittingly forgotten a few, but at my age, that's just how it is.

Probably my very first friend was Henry Bloomstein, whom I've known since I was five years old. Henry and I met in kindergarten in New York City. Even after I changed grade schools we remained the best of friends, our friendship thriving through summer camps and synagogue activities. Throughout our school years, Henry not only reviewed most of my papers, he actually wrote a few as well. He is today living in California and still writing.

Another life-long friend, dating back to kindergarten, was Benji Brown, who sadly passed away in 2018. He and his wife, Fran, a schoolmate of my first wife, Joyce, shared many happy times, and unfortunately some very sad times, with us as well. Fran remains a close friend and is highly respected for the work she does in behalf of the paraplegiac community.

Hillel Gross, or Hillie, as everyone called him, was another boyhood friend. He and I were bunkmates at Camp Maple Lake for years, and later became traveling companions throughout Europe and Israel. Because we both shared a love of opera, Hillie and I formed a devoted two-man fan club of the great Swedish tenor, Johann Jonatan "Jussi" Bjorling. We would follow his tour schedule and catch a live performance wherever and whenever we could. An unforgettable highlight was the time we were both invited backstage after a performance to meet Bjorling, one of the leading operatic singers of the 20th century. It was at this point that we discovered the secret to his calm stage demeanor—a very large tumbler of heavily spiked orange juice.

I met Ephie Propp through my parents who were friendly with him. Ephie, now deceased, was married to Gail Dane, whom I met when she was escorted by Ephie—while the two were just dating—as a guest to my mother's Rosh Hashonah luncheon. Ephie had been a celebrated bachelor living an enviable social life in the U.S. and around Europe, but once he met Gail, he gladly gave it all up, becoming a great husband and a beloved father and step-father. Gail, a brilliant and accomplished woman, is actively involved in business and philanthropy. She has been a great help to me on several projects and remains a wonderful friend and trusted confidante.

One of the most important of my life-long acquaintances, whom I also consider to be a friend, is Rabbi Mordecai Kamenetsky. Our family has been closely connected to three generations of the Kamenetskys, all of whom have guided us through numerous life events both spiritual and secular. Mordecai Kamenetsky has always made himself available when called upon, and despite his being occupied with the running of a thriving Yeshiva, he has always made the time for my family whenever we have needed it. His calm grace under pressure, his wisdom, and his friendship are deeply treasured.

Summer camp at Grossinger's introduced me to another lifelong friend, Armand Lindenbaum. He and his wife, Jeannie, like Joyce and I, were summer residents of Atlantic Beach where both of our families grew up together. Our common interests helped form a tight bond which remains to this day.

Like the Lindenbaums, John and Rebecca Steindecker shared a great deal in common with Joyce and me. John, Armand, and I were something of the Three Musketeers of Atlantic Beach, enjoying idling in each others' company for hours on end, usually on one of our boat docks. I'm happy to say these friendships are still all going strong.

The late Machs (pronounced: Max) Birnbach was a friend from a nearby synagogue that I would occasionally attend. Machs was an avid supporter of the Weitzman Institute, known for its cutting edge medical research in Israel, and succeeded in getting me involved to the point that I was put on the organization's American board of directors. Machs, along with Ephie Propp, Armand Lindenbaum, John Steindecker and me, owned a seating row of our own at the Kchilath Jeshurun Synagogue. A plaque bearing all of our names remains on the bench to this day.

Another friend from those days was Lee Runsdorf. Handsome, athletic, and the life of every party, I will forever be thankful to him for introducing me to the best broker in town, my current wife, Elaine.

Shortly after Elaine and I became a couple, she introduced me to Peter Gottsegen who boarded his horse in the same stable as Elaine's. It wasn't long before Peter and his wife Sue, along with Elaine and me, were going for weekly run-and-jumps all over the beautiful surrounding trail system. These were in addition to the countless hunter paces we attended every fall. A run-and-jump is just what it sounds like. You point your horse at a jump (usually a fence, logs or water), run at it, and jump over. A hunter pace is a little more complicated. A rider will go out the day before the event and set a course of around 10-15 miles, depending on the terrain, that a fox hunter would be likely to traverse if chasing a fox. The course calls for speed as well as the skill needed to ride through woods, across fields, and jump over many natural obstacles. On the following day, pairs go out in teams, ride the prescribed course, and try to match the pace-setter's time. The team that comes the closest wins. It's awesome riding and tons of fun. Elaine and I never won, but Peter and Sue occasionally did. No sour grapes. I just loved the pleasure of being out on our horses with everyone else, so we never really raced for speed, just for the sheer joy it brought us.

While our friendship with the Gottsegens was founded on our mutual love of horses and the fun we had riding, it was sealed by our respect for the kind of people they both are: smart, accomplished, involved, yet completely unaffected and unassuming. Peter, who is blessed with a steel trap memory, taught me many lessons, most of which were delivered with his unmistakable sense of humor. Being the better rider, he liked to give me pointers, in particular: "Keep your heels down, and your p*cker up!" Essential man to man advice when you're in the saddle for hours. Now that we've aged out of the sport, Peter has gotten us involved with the Palm Beach Chamber Music Society, where we happily share his passion for classical music. Sadly, our beloved Sue was an early fatality of the Corona virus, which has left us all reeling.

The Fifth Avenue Synagogue was a natural meeting place, and it was there that I was introduced to Ira Rennert and his wife, Inge, as well as Martin and Renate Zimet, both couples having been good friends of my parents and who ultimately became my good friends as well. They were among the earliest members of the synagogue and remain loyal members to this day. From the day Ira and Inge became members, the Rennert and Hirsch families formed a special bond. The Rennerts have been unflagging supporters of the Synagogue, both financially and spiritually.

Even though I've already discussed my professional relationship with Larry Gross in detail, I can't say enough about how much he has meant to me as a friend. His steady presence in times of crises, his support of both my interests and our mutual endeavors, and his unflagging loyalty and genuine kindness are everything I could ask for and hope to find in a friend. Meeting him was a true blessing in my life. I hold a special place in my heart for both Larry and his wife, Ellen.

One of my few business relationships that evolved into a close personal friendship is the one formed with Francois Houpert. Early in my Welbilt career I met Francois at an industry trade show in Chicago where he was representing the French appliance market. We became close business associates and, ultimately, good friends ever since, arranging to spend time together whenever and wherever possible.

One year, in order to surprise Elaine, Francois and his beautiful wife, Antoinette, met us in Venice to celebrate her birthday. Elaine and I have had the privilege of attending the weddings of two of his children, one of which was held in his country home on the outskirts of the Barbizon artist commune in north-central France. I vividly remember the beautiful simplicity and style of this affair. All the guests, following the bride and groom, formed a procession through the charming French village to the centuries-old church. After we were seated, we were all surprised when the ceremony began with a black gospel choir from Harlem, NYC, that infused amazing energy and spirituality to the exquisite affair. I can still hear and feel the sound of those powerful voices reverberating off the stone walls of the small church. It was definitely one of the most memorable weekends we have ever spent.

Regarding weekends spent together, the record for this activity must be held by Ed and Judy Prager. Ed is not merely a friend, but a relative as well. His grandfather, Pincus Hirsch, was the brother of my grandfather, Louis Hirsch. Pincus had 5 daughters, one of whom, Molly, was Ed's mother. We're both not sure exactly what our relationship is called, but we're definitely cousins of some degree. Ed and Judy are great people—fun to be with, excellent company, and if you ever need anything fixed, Ed's your man!

Through my philanthropic work with the Israel Development Corporation (State of Israel Bonds), I was very fortunate to meet Israel "Izzy" Tapoohi and his wife Regina. From our first meeting it was obvious that we thought alike and that our personalities dovetailed, making us a formidable team. Together we were able to achieve record results for Bonds, and in the process we became great friends. Luckily Elaine and Regina enjoy each others' company as much as Izzy and I do, so we still try to spend as many weekends and evenings together as time and travel will allow.

Although we've only known each other for a few years, thanks to our mutual involvement with Israel Bonds, I now count Robert Issenman and his wife, Lise, as our good friends. They live in Montreal, with a winter escape in Naples, Florida, so we don't get to see them as often as we'd like, but thanks to our regular contact via email, we have gotten to know each other and have become involved with each others' families. Elaine and I truly enjoy their company and hope our friendship continues to grow and flourish.

Moving to Palm Beach opened up another world of friendships, some with people whom I had known from New York, but, in Florida, I found I was able to take such relationships to new levels. One such person, whom I had known for years through the Fifth Avenue Synagogue, is Larry Friedland, a true mensch and a great all around human being. We share interests in business, family, and a love of our homes in Palm Beach, pinching ourselves for our good fortune to have landed in such an amazing place. As the years go by, Elaine and I grow closer and more fond of Larry and his wife, Marilyn, as well as with their beautiful family.

I have known the Barnetts for many years through the Fifth Avenue Synagogue, but we have truly cemented our relationship in Palm Beach. Victor and his wife, Lainie, are the most gracious of hosts, able to effortlessly assemble colleagues from their careers along with friends they have met through their travels around the world. Among other credits to her name, Lainie was the longest serving president of Legal Services Corporation in Washington D. C., and remains a hard-working, fearless proponent of legal rights for the elderly and disadvantaged. Victor, a retired "Captain of Industry," is an avid collector of exquisite glass art and antiquities.

I actually met Steven Stern through my brother David, since they had been college roommates at Cornell. While I had always enjoyed his company, it wasn't until we both wound up living in Palm Beach that Elaine and I really got to know Steve and his wife, Bonnie. Steve—always pragmatic and insightful—and I share similar philosophies when it comes to philanthropy, politics, and synagogues, while Elaine and Bonnie tackle everything else. We love spending time with both of them at their stunning home.

Another family friend with whom I reconnected in Palm Beach is Dr. Mal Dorman, a friend of our family for more than 60 years. Mal is not only a great surgeon, having saved countless lives in his long and distinguished career, he's also a wonderful person whose life mission is helping people. I'm truly lucky to count him as a good friend.

In Palm Beach I also re-united with two other married couples, both old friends from New York and Atlantic Beach. Edith Greenfield and her husband Joe, who unfortunately died in 2018, had both been friends of my parents. Before we were quarantined by the Corona virus, we would see each other frequently since we live in the same building. But even a quarantine hasn't slowed Edith down. I gratefully enjoy regular calls from her each week—conversations marked by her true pearls of wisdom and sage advice.

My other re-kindled friendship is with Danny Abraham, undoubtedly one of America's greatest philanthropists. It's because of Danny that I am involved with the Mayo Clinic, where Danny is revered for having contributed so much to the quality of the lives of the professionals who work there. He and I now share other interests as well, and are presently working together on a project to combat antisemitism on South Florida high school campuses. Elaine has a great relationship with his smart and beautiful wife, Ewa (pronounced: Eva), and we are so fortunate to spend many evenings together these days.

Ric Smith and his wife, Sandy, are new friends whom we met shortly after moving to Palm Beach. Ric is smart, fun, kind, generous, and a strong advocate for everything he believes in. He is also a great husband, a doting grandfather to Leo, and my sidekick for many of my philanthropic projects. He's the very definition of dependable and I'm truly glad he's become part of our lives.

Danny Baldinger had been such a profound part of my life—a constant friend and companion—that I no longer recall exactly when or where we met. I can truly say that he was my best friend. For many years, a day rarely passed without the two of us calling or seeing one another. Our friendship thrived through both my marriages. Joyce and I spent many happy times with Danny and his wife, Margie, and later Elaine and I continued to do the same.

Danny was the CEO of Louis Baldinger & Sons, a manufacturer of lighting fixtures founded by his grandfather. Danny and I played doubles tennis as a team summer after summer and were avid fitness runners for many years, always trying to help keep each other in good shape. When I was president of Maimonides Medical Center, I appointed Danny to oversee the nursing department, where he was beloved by the staff because of his magnanimous personality and great sense of humor.

Danny was responsible for my singular public performance as a musician. He had been a member of the marching band while attending Syracuse University and every year would return to march with the alumni across the football field during the game's half time presentation. One year, Danny convinced me to come along with him, shoved a piccolo into my hands, and then snuck me onto the field where I marched along behind him, pretending to play. We laughed about that for years.

Once, when I was still married to Joyce, Danny and I found that we had separate business meetings in Las Vegas, after which we decided to get together and take a day off to visit the Grand Canyon in Arizona. We planned to fly home together after our sight-seeing tour, since we both had to get home and meet our wives at a formal event we were both committed to attend. We arranged our flights, leaving us plenty of time after arriving home to change into formal attire and make it to the event. When Danny and I got to the Grand Canyon we decided to take one of the mule trips being offered. Unfortunately the trip ran later than expected, so we rushed to the airport, dressed in boots and jeans, only to miss our plane. We were able to catch the next one, but it arrived too late for us to stop at home to change clothes, so we were forced to show up at the formal affair looking like two crazy cowpokes, boots, hats, and all. It was, by far, the best black-tie event we ever attended.

Everyone knew Danny loved to cook, and every year he looked forward to hosting his famed Red, White, and Blue dinner. Only food in those colors was served, and it was unbelievable how clever and creative Danny was, year after year, at producing menus to meet those demanding specifications. Not surprisingly, the dinner was always held in their summer home on the Fourth of July. As fate would have it, Danny died on July 4, 2007. I miss my dear old friend every day and hope that wherever he is, he's saving a place for me.

Richard L. Hirsch

CHAPTER THIRTEEN
TIKKUN OLAM

At the podium.

"If you want happiness for a year, inherit a fortune. If you want happiness for a lifetime, help someone else."
–Confucius

The Hebrew word "*Tzedakah*" is most commonly translated as "charity," but this is not its true meaning. It actually means "Justice" or "Righteousness." It is not understood, in Judaic terms, to be a voluntary or optional act of generosity. Rather *Tzedakah* is an ethical obligation to "do the right thing."

Unlike conventional charity, Tzedakah is a *"mitzvah"* or commandment that must be carried out by everyone, regardless of one's financial standing, and is intended to benefit the giver as well as the recipient. During the Middle Ages, the great Jewish sage and teacher, Maimonides, developed an eight-level hierarchy of *Tzedakah*. The highest form is to give a gift that will result in the recipient becoming self-sufficient and no longer needing assistance. It is better to give a hungry man a fishing pole than a fish, according to that great Rabbinic scholar, Confucius.

As explained earlier, I grew up as part of a family that deeply cherished such values. I was immersed in a culture of caring that instilled within me a gut level instinct to engage in *Tzedakah*. This attribute is embedded in my DNA and a key component of who I am today.

I likewise have always embraced the Talmudic concept of *"Tikkun Olam"* or the repairing of the world. As Jews, we are commanded to do whatever we can to make the world a better place for others. While many these days have taken this term to be a rallying cry for causes promoting social justice, I do not believe that view represents its original intent. *Tikkun Olam* is simply the goal, the desired outcome, of all people fulfilling the mitzvah of *Tzedakah*. The troubles of this world can be repaired, we are taught, through acts of righteousness and loving kindness. This is the credo that I was taught to believe and the one that I have attempted to pass on to my family.

I must admit that there were times in my life when I was forced to question our family's deep commitment to philanthropy. I recall one episode that took place shortly after I took over the leadership of Welbilt in the early 1970's. My father, Henry, as has been noted, was a strong supporter of a Jewish school called Yeshiva Torah Vodaath. At this point our company was enduring losses and I was engaged in a desperate attempt to keep it from going south. I approached my father, whom I regarded as being generous to a fault, and made my pitch.

"We need to cut back on the philanthropy, Dad," I explained. "We're experiencing operational losses so we get no tax benefits from these charitable contributions. I'm thinking we tell YTV (Yeshiva Torah Vodaath) that we will have to cut back on our commitments to them."

My father would not hear of it. He responded by listing the important work they were carrying out to build a strong Jewish community. "This is our future, Richard," he said. "We can never abandon our future." I understood at that moment that my father's devotion to the Jewish people overshadowed his commitment to his own financial prosperity. I came to understand and accept this viewpoint as, over the coming years, we continued to extend our support to the yeshiva. One of the buildings that today houses YTV's main campus bears the names of my grandparents, Louis and Esther Hirsch, as a tribute to my father's unflagging generosity.

I witnessed both of my parents give and give and give of both their time and their wealth and I learned from them that acts of generosity should not be connected to enhancing one's own wealth or social status, but to the meaning it brings to your life.

Over the course of my life, I have continued to carry on our family's support for the outstanding work of Yeshiva Torah Vodaath, just as I and my siblings have done on behalf of Fifth Avenue Synagogue and other worthy institutions. I am pleased to report that the synagogue my father established still adheres today to the founding principles he championed. Henry Hirsch wanted to create a synagogue that was more than merely a space for prayer. His understanding of a true House of Prayer was based on the small community *shteibels* prevalent in pre-war Eastern Europe. These were not grand synagogues housed in imposing Gothic structures, but were often set up in small private homes where the men were packed in so tightly they could sway together in unison as they "*davened*" (prayed). While my father sought an intimate and warm atmosphere that was conducive to prayer and learning, he wanted it housed in an elegant setting befitting his friends and that would appeal to the up-and-coming modern Jewish community. It has been our family's happy obligation and our legacy to continue to support his vision.

During the Depression, federal income tax was negligible and the notion of making charitable gifts to reduce your taxes didn't yet exist. Naturally, his generous nature made my father something of a soft touch during those years. At that time, he was not yet a captain of industry with vast wealth. He ran an enameling company that made cooking ranges. He was just like a lot of other Jewish fellows who emerged from the New York immigrant community and were running successful businesses. Yet, when it came time to find a donor, an underwriter, a sponsor, or an angel, they lined up at Henry Hirsch's door.

The following story illustrates this point. The year was 1936 as Hitler was rising to power in Germany. My father was approached by the renowned Hungarian-born rabbi, Shraga Feivel Mendlowitz, who was likely introduced to him by my father's close friend Harry Hershkowitz. Rabbi Mendlowitz was a leader of American Orthodoxy who had established such key institutions as Torah U'Mesorah and in 1921 had helped to found Yeshiva Torah Vodaath in Brooklyn.

At one point, referring to Torah Vodaath, the rabbi implored my father: "Henry, we need a camp for all these Jewish children. They've never seen a tree!"

My father didn't respond with: "I'll discuss this with our charitable giving committee." He didn't question: "Where's the money going to come from to operate the camp?" What he did was ask: "How much do you need?" He then wrote the Rabbi a check on the spot for $20,000 or roughly the equivalent of $370,000 in 2020 dollars. The yeshiva used the money to buy the property in Highland New York and established America's first Jewish summer camp.

To support the camp's operations, my parents created the Rose Getelson Sunshine Fund, named after my maternal grandmother. This name was selected because of my mother's deep involvement in the creation and operation of the camp. The facility, dubbed Camp Mesivta, operated for many years and produced it's share of well-known personalities and successful businessmen. The camp no longer exists but in its place today stands an outstanding school which is still supported by our family.

My father was deeply influenced by Rabbi Mendlowitz whose worldview was informed by *Torah im Derech Eretz*. This term refers to observing the teachings of the Holy Torah while at the same time interacting with the general society. It is a position adopted in contrast to the insulated and cloistered communities found in the Chassidic world. At his death in 1948, it was said by many that if it were not for Rabbi Mendlowitz this Yeshiva would not have come into existence. It should be added that it was my father, and other like-minded philanthropists working quietly in the background, who made it financially possible for the esteemed rabbi to achieve such impressive outcomes.

Patronage vs. Participatory Philanthropy

The tradition of giving that I inherited from my parents consisted of two components. Patronage and Participation. The first involved merely extending financial support, while the second added to this a full engagement in the affairs and fortunes of the beneficiary institution. In the case of my father, it was into this second "involved" group that such organizations as the Fifth Avenue Synagogue and Yeshiva Torah Vodaath fell. This distinction is demonstrated in the following anecdote.

The prime minister of Israel was once making an official visit to a newly opened library in Tel Aviv.

"Welcome, Mr. Prime Minister, to the Lefkovitz Library," said his tour guide as she ushered him through the front doors. The prime minister took her aside and whispered:

"Please help me out here. Who is this Lefkovitz?"

"Oh," she replied. "He is a great writer."

"I see," he said. "What did he write?"

"A big check."

It is the second, or Participation category that I feel embodies the true essence of philanthropy and so, I have likewise divided my giving into these two realms. The work of the first, or Patronage category, has been carried out via the various charitable foundations that I and my family members have established over the years. The first of these, the Louis and Esther Hirsch Foundation, was created in the 1930's and named after my grandparents. It was changed to the Henry and Myrtle Hirsch Family Foundation in 1947 and has endured through 2020, dispensing financial support for a multitude of worthy causes, both Jewish and secular. The Foundation is directed by me and my two siblings (David Hirsch and Carole Friedman) along with my son, Adam; my nephew, Jason; and my niece, Debbie Cooper.

A look at a handful of the many organizations that received major gifts from the Henry and Myrtle Hirsch Family Foundation in recent years demonstrates the direction and diversity of our family's giving. These include: The Women's International Zionist Organization, the Metropolitan Opera, the Fifth Avenue Synagogue, CLAL, Yeshiva Kehilath Yakov, Columbia University Department of Optometry, and many more.

As explained earlier, my siblings and I have carried on the tradition of "hands-on" involvement with my father's pet Participation projects, such as the Fifth Avenue Synagogue (see Chapter Five), which he and noted German-born philanthropist, Hermann Merkin, founded in the 1950's. I have continued to be an active participant in overseeing my father's interest in the synagogue, and am proud to say that I have also experienced this deeper level of involvement with other worthy organizations in the intervening years. Perhaps a case study would best illustrate this point.

A key example of my moving from Patronage to Participatory philanthropy involves the Maimonides Medical Center in Borough Park, Brooklyn. I was first introduced to the hospital by its board chairman, Dave Wassner. Two active board members, Benjamin Eisenstadt (the inventor of Sweet 'n Low sugar substitute) and Al Schreiber (who would go on to be the longest-serving chairman of the Maimonides board) worked hard to enlist my participation in support of the hospital. I agreed and, at first, became strictly a financial supporter of this outstanding non-profit and non-sectarian organization. However, with the loss of my son, Larry, my involvement with the institution moved up to the next level. Shortly after Larry's death in 1972, I decided to make a gift to the hospital that resulted in the naming of a room in the emergency center in his memory. At this point I started becoming more involved with Maimonides as I learned more about its impressive history.

Maimonides Medical Center was created in 1947 in much the same way as new synagogues are formed: via the merger of United Israel Zion and Beth Moses Hospitals. It bears the name of Rabbi Moshe Ben Maimon, a 12th century sage, philosopher and doctor also known as the Rambam. Today, the hospital, along with the Montefiore Medical Center, is affiliated with Yeshiva University's Albert Einstein College of Medicine.

As a result of my growing level of support, the hospital's chairman, Dave Wassner, took me under his wing and invited me to accept a seat on its governing board. Tragically, Dave was killed shortly thereafter in an auto accident that occurred, ironically, not far from the hospital. This created a leadership vacancy which was first filled by Ben Eisenstadt and then by me. I soon found myself deeply involved in the operation of the hospital.

What I discovered upon becoming chairman in the late 1980's was quite disturbing. The hospital itself was bleeding money despite the fact that its maternity ward was delivering more babies than any other hospital in America. I started delving into the day-to-day operations with a vengeance and, because I was a businessman and not a physician, I was able to make an accurate diagnosis: If immediate measures were not taken, this patient was terminal. Putting those measures into place became almost a full-time job for me. Rescuing the hospital, which fortunately was located not far from my office in Maspeth, Queens, became my new challenge.

I worked closely with the administration and discovered that they had been neglecting the enormous fund-raising opportunities that lay before them. Some of the most prominent and well-to-do citizens of Brooklyn and elsewhere had been patients at Maimonides, yet there had been little follow-up with this wealthy demographic to solicit their financial support. This situation was addressed, and soon donations began to come in. Once that process began, I was able to use my connections with the banking and financial world, specifically the First Pennsylvania Bank in Philadelphia, to work out the hospital's debt and begin to put it on a sound financial footing for the long-term.

As I pored over the hospital's financial records, I noted that there were certain areas of the operation that—were they to be isolated from the overall picture—could be considered as profit centers. Among these were the ambulance service and the pharmacy. If I considered the revenue against the expenses of just these two divisions, the hospital would be operating in the black. Harkening to my experience at Welbilt, where I had granted a great deal of autonomy to the company's myriad divisions, I developed a plan to surgically spin off these healthy, profitable departments from the ailing total operation. Although I had a tough time convincing the hospital accountants, I finally prevailed in isolating both the pharmacy and the ambulance service as separate, wholly-owned entities. This led to improving the overall credit rating of the hospital and opened the door to obtaining affordable financing that made a restructuring possible. It was a key step towards eventually achieving financial solvency for Maimonides.

All this was going on during a period of historic break-throughs in the field of cardiac surgery. I knew that back in 1961, the world's first pacemaker was developed at Maimonides, but the hospital had not kept up the pace in terms of innovation in this area since then. The board felt it would benefit the hospital's reputation if we could attract some cutting edge cardio-surgeons to join its research laboratory. In this vein, we sought out and succeeded—in 1982—to convince a leading cardiologist, Dr. Joseph N. Cunningham, Jr., to move from NYU to Maimonides. Cunningham, who died suddenly at age 70 in 2001, was a colorful figure who headed the hospital's cardiac center for nearly two decades. He was a beloved, dynamic and forward-thinking leader who launched numerous strategic initiatives during his tenure. A truly larger-than-life figure, Joe was perhaps best remembered by the hospital staff for the yearly parties at his upstate New York farm that featured hayrides and T-shirts bearing his "Swamp Fox" nickname.

These efforts at upgrading the hospital's staffing profile and financial footing succeeded in rescuing Maimonides from the brink and transforming it into one of the premier and most respected medical facilities in New York. Whereas it remains a top venue for new births, by the early 2000's, the New York Times reported that in an analysis of 5000 hospitals by the US Department of Health and Human Services, Maimonides was listed as one of the five hospitals with the lowest mortality rate in the nation. Today, Maimonides ranks among the top five percent of hospitals for overall quality outcomes according to the HealthGrades rating service. It is considered one of the top hospitals in New York State in the areas of cardiology, coronary intervention, stroke treatment and gastrointestinal medical services.

Another example of the type of "hands on" philanthropy I have practiced involves a newspaper called The Jewish Week. I had originally become involved with the paper at the encouragement of four Jewish community leaders, Eugene Grant, Mort Kornriech, Lawrence Kobrin and Robert Arnow. Born as a tiny tabloid in the late 1970's, The Jewish Week was then produced out of a small New York City office containing three typewriters and a ticker-tape machine. By the 1990's, the weekly publication had grown to become a highly regarded media outlet known for its top-level reporting, its diverse analysis and powerful opinion pieces. The award-winning paper was serving as the primary distribution channel for relevant news to the Jewish community in the metropolitan New York City area. It enjoyed a paid circulation at the time of more than fifty thousand and had been replicated in Jewish communities across America.

While it sold advertising to vendors seeking to target the New York Jewish community, these ads alone did not generate sufficient revenue to keep the paper afloat. Since it was regarded as a key community asset, the paper had been receiving an annual subsidy from the local Jewish Federation. This subsidy peaked at $1.2 million before declining fundraising revenues forced the Federation to cut its level of support. At the same time, advertising revenue began to decline as other types of media competed for advertisers' dollars.

At that point I was asked to increase my level of involvement in order to help find a financial solution. Federation was then providing only about one million dollars per year and the paper was facing imminent collapse unless private donors could be found to cover the shortfall. But, there was a problem, they explained. The newspaper was a business, not a 501(c)(3) not-for-profit organization. Any money gifted to the paper directly would not qualify as a deductible charitable contribution. This would have a serious impact on the willingness of some potential donors to make a gift.

It was during this time that the Jewish Week board was building content for the development of various educational programs. These became the perfect vehicles for funders to direct their charitable donations towards the Jewish Week. The programs were successful enough to bring in the necessary revenues and also to attract a vibrant, young, new audience.

One of these new programs, introduced in 2002, was a not-for-profit entity known as Write-On For Israel. It was designed as an educational initiative whose mission was to promote journalism training for high school Juniors and Seniors. Another of these initiatives was Fresh Ink For Teens, an online program for high school students around the globe that publishes articles from students on topics about the teenage Jewish experience. Thanks to proper promotion and public relations, Write-On For Israel and the others were able to attract charitable contributions from across the New York Jewish philanthropic community. The newspaper operation was then able to off-load a number of its expenses, thereby lowering its operating budget and bringing it back into solvency.

Today, Write-On For Israel serves as one of the first "early engagement" programs to identify and educate young Jewish leaders in high school before they get to the college campus. This program provides them with the defensive tools they need to combat BDS

(Boycott, Divest, Sanction) and other forms of campus anti-semitism. Its highly selective leadership training program targets top high school Juniors and Seniors who share a deep connection to Judaism and a desire to become active and vocal leaders of the pro-Israel movement on campus. Their primary tool is journalism. These Write-On students are trained to apply their writing skills when they arrive on campus toward defending and advocating for Israel. I am extremely proud to have been one of the founders of outstanding, public programs like this for the benefit of the Jewish Community.

The guiding force at the Jewish Week since we hired him in 1993 has been Gary Rosenblatt, who retired in 2020. At the time we convinced him to come aboard, Gary had been enjoying an exemplary career for nearly 20 years at America's largest circulation Jewish newspaper at the time, the Baltimore Jewish Times. We explained to Gary about the dire situation we were facing at the NY Jewish Week and convinced him to be our white knight. I was delighted when he agreed. His leadership was a key ingredient in our rescue of the New York Jewish Week. Although my active participation in the paper's operations ended in 2015, I still retain a seat on the board and follow its fortunes closely.

While the majority of my philanthropic giving is centered around the family foundations mentioned, I am also deeply involved with a non-family foundation for which I serve as chairman. The story of the Morty and Gloria Wolosoff Foundation is twisted, intriguing, and proved to be one of my most difficult assignments.

Morty Wolosoff was a self-made real estate developer who died in New York's Mt. Sinai Hospital at age 87 shortly after the 9/11 attacks. He was a close friend of my father's and shared many of his same philanthropic affections. Morty was a boating enthusiast who had owned several luxury yachts, one of which was custom built for him and sank in a storm as it was being delivered for its maiden voyage. His love of the sea led to his having built the nation's largest covered marina in St. Petersburg, FL. One day, a few years before he died, Morty asked me join him for a walk in Central Park. I obliged and we soon found ourselves chatting on a secluded park bench.

"Richard," he said, "I have been noticing the way you manage your family's charities. I like the way you have continued to support the Fifth Avenue synagogue and your father's other favorite causes after he died." I thanked him for the kind words.

"I want you to do the same for me." He pointed out that his health was not the best and that he had no one he felt he could rely upon to be sure that his money would be spent on charities that mattered to him after he was gone. His daughter, Wendy, his only child, had no involvement at all in his foundation, Morty explained. He asked for my help, and, of course, I agreed.

I convinced him to join me on a trip to Israel to see some of the projects in which I was involved. We both had a great time since we shared many of the same passions and interests. It proved to be a very productive trip, and we both returned invigorated, energized, and filled with enthusiasm

The next thing we did was have me added as trustee to his foundation, with the intention of my assuming all responsibilities for the management of all assets and distributions upon his death. At that point, all his assets were to go to his wife and then flow to the Foundation upon her death. During that year, Morty would send me the various charities he wanted to support and I would see that each one received a gift from the Morty and Gloria Family Foundation. Then Morty died and things began to get complicated.

Morty's wife, Gloria had developed a close relationship with a certain Worth Avenue jewelry merchant in Palm Beach. As soon as Gloria took control of the estate, she turned over all the assets to her companion. Naturally this brought about a strong reaction from both Morty's daughter, Wendy, and from me, since I had been entrusted by Morty to make sure this type of thing did not happen. Unfortunately Gloria was sinking into dementia which led to some very bad decisions being made, creating serious complications when it came to settling the estate.

Wendy, an astrological counselor and transpersonal psychologist, was outraged, but not in a financial position to challenge her mother's behavior. In the name of the Foundation, I took immediate legal steps to block Gloria's actions. Having the financial means to do so, Gloria assembled a gold-plated team of top white shoe lawyers to defend her right to subvert her late husband's wishes. I, in turn, contacted a trusted and capable New York attorney, David M. Olasov who acted swiftly and brilliantly in crafting a very strong case. The battle lines had been drawn.

"If she's allowed to get away with this," I explained to David, "it will mean the Foundation gets nothing and those charities Morty cared about will get screwed." David understood immediately.

"You say she handed over an inheritance worth tens of millions to her jeweler?" he asked.

"Yeah. Nuts, isn't it?"

"It sure is and that's our case. Nobody in their right mind would do such a thing and the fact that she did it proves that she is not legally capable of managing the estate. We will ask the court to appoint a competent receiver and we should be able to get that done."

David's encouraging words were welcome, but it would be a long and arduous trail that would not fully come to resolution till Gloria's death in 2009. David guided us patiently and expertly through the complex legalities, and in the end we were able to protect the estate and get things back on track. A settlement was finally reached after which we recovered a sizable amount of the estate's assets for the Foundation. Regrettably, after deducting the legal fees from the amount, at the end of the day the jeweler wound up receiving the largest chunk of the proceeds..

Since then I have done my utmost to see that the Morty and Gloria Wolosoff Foundation carry on it's giving in the manner that Morty would have wished. The Foundation today still holds a sizable sum in assets. As the years roll by, the question of who will manage this Foundation, as well as the others mentioned previously, becomes more and more challenging.

One final example of an organization to which I directed more than my money is an entity that has helped to finance the infrastructure of the Israeli economy since the 1950's. The State of Israel Bonds was established by David Ben Gurion in the early days of the Jewish nation. Its mission is to sell financial debt obligations around the world to finance the building of roads, bridges, power plants, and other non-military government projects. I had grown up hearing about Israel Bonds and had often purchased their bearer bond certificates for my investment portfolio. They paid a competitive rate of return and had never defaulted or even delayed a payment. But it wasn't until I was approached by venerated New York developer and philanthropist, Eugene Grant, that my level of involvement moved into the Participation zone.

Grant, whom everyone called Gene, had been one of the four men who had convinced me to become involved with the Jewish Week. He had been born Eugene Greenberg in Hell's Kitchen, New York during the first World War. Building on his father's real estate business, Gene founded his fortune by building housing for returning veterans after World War II. He eventually wound up owning St. John's Terminal and the old Saks building at 34th and Broadway. Gene was a very close friend and a true Renaissance man. Not only was he a brilliant and successful businessman, he was also a gifted pianist who performed for our guests at my 60th birthday party, held at New York's sorely-missed Four Seasons Restaurant. Gene was an avid sportsman who had, while in his early 80's, portaged a canoe to retrace the original Louis and Clark trail. Among his many philanthropic activities was his saving of the city of Venice and all the art treasures that entailed. But Gene's interests were not limited to high culture. He was also a die-hard Michigan University alumnus. At his urging, he, my son, Adam (also an MU alum), Elaine and I joined him at the 100th RoseBowl game in 2014 where we rooted his Spartans on to a 24 to 20 victory over the Stanford Cardinals.

Gene was a pillar of the Jewish community up until his death at age 99 in 2018. It was during his tenure as president of UJA-Federation of New York, that he approached me about becoming involved with Israel Bonds.

I joined the Bonds board in 1998, became vice-president in 2007, and was named president in 2010. During my vice presidency there was a major shift in Israel Bonds direction, and about a year after I assumed the presidency, a dynamic new president, Izzy Tapoohi, was appointed. Prior to joining Israel Bonds, Tapoohi, an Australian business leader, had headed Bezeq, Israel's largest telecommunications provider and had also served in top-level advisory positions in the Netanyahu governments. I got to know Izzy and was inspired by his vision for Israel Bonds. Together, we worked closely with the Israeli Finance Ministry in charting successful Bond sale campaigns in the U.S. and Europe.

Tapoohi moved on from Israel Bonds in 2016 to head the Israel Foundation, the organization responsible for the Birthright Israel program that provides young North Americans with free visits to Israel. My involvement in Israel Bonds began to decline at this point and, while I remain a strong supporter and investor in the movement, I tendered my resignations as Domestic Division Chairman in 2019 and as International Division Chairman in 2020. Here are some excerpts from my departure remarks delivered to the Board at that time:

"I am announcing my retirement from all Israel Bond activities at the end of this morning's meeting and before the election of new officers.

We are all concerned about the current political environment in Israel. Unfortunately, the delay of the Israeli elections affects the finance ministry staffing. There are a number of situations that concern me which should be addressed as you go forward.

One of these relates to the interaction between our domestic division, the DCI, and our international division. The numbers reveal underperformance. The cost of operations has continued to grow while bond sales have remained stagnant.

At a time when antisemitism and anti-Zionism are becoming rampant in our core communities and schools, when security at our educational and recreational facilities is taking a financial toll, these Israeli dollar expenditures could be better spent in those areas, here and around the world, that are on the front lines facing these very real threats to our existence.

For the last two years I have been spending my time and money on U.S. high schools and college campuses, learning and studying these issues in order to understand how we can help our youth to cope with antisemitism and to formulate a path to change."

My words reflected the direction that I was moving towards in terms of my future philanthropy. I have become convinced that the future of American Jewry lies in the hands of our young people. This is why I have become increasingly involved—on not merely a Patronage level, but on a Participation level—with organizations like NCSY. NCSY is the world-recognized youth division of the Orthodox Union that has played a pivotal role in the lives of Jewish teenagers since 1951. Its mission is to build, among Jewish teens, a strong connection to their roots and traditions through inspiration and leadership skills.

One of their key programs is the JSU, or Jewish Student Union, that sets up branches in the nation's high schools to build awareness about Israel and Jewish culture. I am likewise working closely with Brown University Hillel these days to establish a student-directed program that will serve to combat antisemitism on our nation's college campuses. It is through the active and involved support of organizations like these that I hope to fulfill the mission of my people known as *Tikkun Olam*. It is via such support that I seek to contribute to what I envision as a bright enduring future for the Jewish people.

Chapter Fourteen
Thinking Ahead

(l-r) Me with my sister, Carole, and my brother, David in 2015 holding a photo of our younger selves taken 60 years earlier in 1955.

"Being the richest man in the cemetary doesn't matter to me. Going to bed at night saying we've done something wonderful...that's what matters to me."

–Steve Jobs

This book is being written in 2020 in the midst of the Coronavirus pandemic that is holding the world in its grip. Of all the industries that are being hit hard by the economic impact of the virus, none is more devastating to the daily lives of the average person than the restaurant and food service sector. Given my long years of active involvement in the area, I am frequently called upon by industry leaders for my opinion about what lies ahead for these businesses in the coming post-pandemic world. While the depth of my experience may make my crystal ball a bit clearer than most, so much of what happens will depend on how long the virus remains unstoppable and on how deep the economic fallout becomes. For what it's worth, I will share my current thinking on this topic with you.

First, the hard facts. By the time the pandemic has run its course, it's likely that more than one third of the world's restaurants will be forced to restructure or close their operations. The dining habits of millions of people are undergoing radical change and as such will present even more challenges to an already beleaguered industry. Particularly hard hit will be the smaller independent businesses and franchisees who, no pun intended, run hand-to-mouth operations, and do not typically have the cash reserves to sustain them for long periods of forced closure.

I foresee that these stark realities are going to present significant opportunities for the large-scale operators. As a result of this shake-out, these companies will see their market shares grow and their control and influence expand in the coming years. With the widespread closings of family casual, bistro venues, and up-scale restaurants, the fast-food sector, with it's nimble operations and low capital requirements, will be more easily able to meet the pent-up demand created by the massive closings happening around them.

As Albert Einstein, probably the greatest problem-solver of all time, once said: "In the middle of difficulty lies opportunity." The massive restaurant closings and restructurings will lead to a flood of high-quality used restaurant equipment being dumped on the market. Much of this, along with the inevitable foreclosed real estate, will end up in the hands of lenders who will be forced to repossess financed equipment because of the owner's default. The glut will drive down prices across the board, thus representing a unique opportunity for the savvy.

In addition to my take on business matters, my counsel has also been solicited in the area of Jewish community affairs, particularly in the wake of my recent departure from my position as International Chairman of State of Israel Bonds. My opinion, based on careful observation, is that the recent interminable election process in Israel that finally resulted in a coalition government after 17 months of limbo, had a devastating effect on the nation. In particular, the Israel Bond organization that operates under the authority of the Israeli Finance Ministry, was caught in a quagmire under the lame duck leadership that prevailed during that period.

This tremendous delay in forming a functioning government affected not only the Finance Ministry and Bonds, but it also created an enormous leadership void that impacted all aspects of Jewish life. Israel is still paying the price for that extended lapse. The question now becomes: "How do they correct this systemic problem in order to avoid its recurrence?"

When the state was born under David Ben-Gurion in 1948, the new nation adopted the existing governmental structure based on the colonial power that had been there for the prior 70 years, known as the British mandate. Israel thus inherited the British parliamentary system of government under which the prime minister, the nation's head of state, is selected based on the party that holds the majority of seats in the Parliament—known as the Knesset in Israel. This was a mistake at the time and one that haunts the country today, resulting in the recent fiasco.

Under Israel's current system, the electorate is divided into a few large parties and many smaller ones, none of which are able to form the legislative majority needed in order to govern without forming unholy coalitions with other parties. Forming such coalitions proved next to impossible after the last election, requiring a Coronavirus outbreak to finally make it happen. If the pandemic had not come along, they would probably still be holding futile elections, and still be unable to form a governing coalition.

I feel the solution lies in a radical overhaul of the entire system of governance, adopting instead a constitutional system like we have in the United States. While our system has its share of shortcomings, it has endured and operated effectively for nearly 250 years. It is not mere chauvinism that prompts me to suggest this, but a sincere desire to see Israel flourish and succeed without any future repetitions of this devastating leadership crisis.

One factor that has exacerbated the problem in Israel is the absence of comprehensive leadership in the American Jewish philanthropic community. At one time this role fell to the Conference of Presidents of Major Jewish Organizations. This entity served as a sanctioning body and provided legitimation and its imprimatur to those 501(c)(3) Jewish organizations it deemed worthy. Today, the Conference of Presidents has become ineffective, either unable or unwilling to properly vet the large numbers of Jewish organizations that have entered the philanthropic arena. As the number of such organizations has grown significantly, they are increasingly forced to compete against one another for donations from the same donors for the same causes. This competition has weakened the ability of many of them to achieve their goals. I feel that if the Conference of Presidents could be re-organized, it could consolidate the power and influence of these organizations. Such a move would render their operations more efficient, more effective, and ultimately generate more participation among not only American Jews, but among the steadily growing numbers of Israeli Jews of means as well.

The irony of this problem lies in the fact that due to its history and culture, Israel does not have a tradition of philanthropy, which is surprising considering the essential concept of *Tzedakah* engrained in Jewish traditions. Serious fund-raising efforts that target the Israeli or Israeli-American population, often fall on deaf ears. This despite the fact that the number of Israeli millionaires is growing rapidly as the "Start-Up Nation" continues to create successful new companies in the fields of information technology, pharmaceuticals, telecommunications, medical devices, cyber-security, and others.

In light of how successful and wealthy Israel is becoming, the focus of American philanthropic organizations needs to undergo a paradigm shift towards the challenges we are facing here at home. These include feeding our hungry and needy, education of our youth, insuring the continuity of Jewish culture and tradition, helping the remaining Holocaust survivors, and dealing with anti-semitism in all its forms. It's time for Americans to look inward, as well as outward.

These are the lessons that I have learned, and lived, and that have informed who I am today. As for my children and grandchildren, I urge you to never abandon your deep historic and familial traditions. You are descended from extraordinary families, and are now blessed with extraordinary families of your own. I hope that my story and the stories of our forebears will serve as the impetus for your own successes, not just for material comforts, but to advance the well-being of our community. As you build your lives and live your dreams, never forget that the two basic principles of charity (*Tzedakah*) and healing the world (*Tikkun Olam*), should always serve as the foundations of your lives.

Remember the gifts you are lucky to have received: a great family, a great upbringing by loving parents, a great education, and a great country, America, that allows you immense freedoms, including, most importantly, the freedom of religion. The price of your privilege is not free, however. The cost is your responsibility, and the greater the privilege, the higher the cost. Never forget that privilege entails responsibility.

As mega-entrepreneur, Richard Branson, said," My attitude has always been, if you fall flat on your face, at least you're moving forward. All you have to do is get back up and try again." Or as I like to say, "Sempre Avanti!"

Richard L. Hirsch

Family Tree

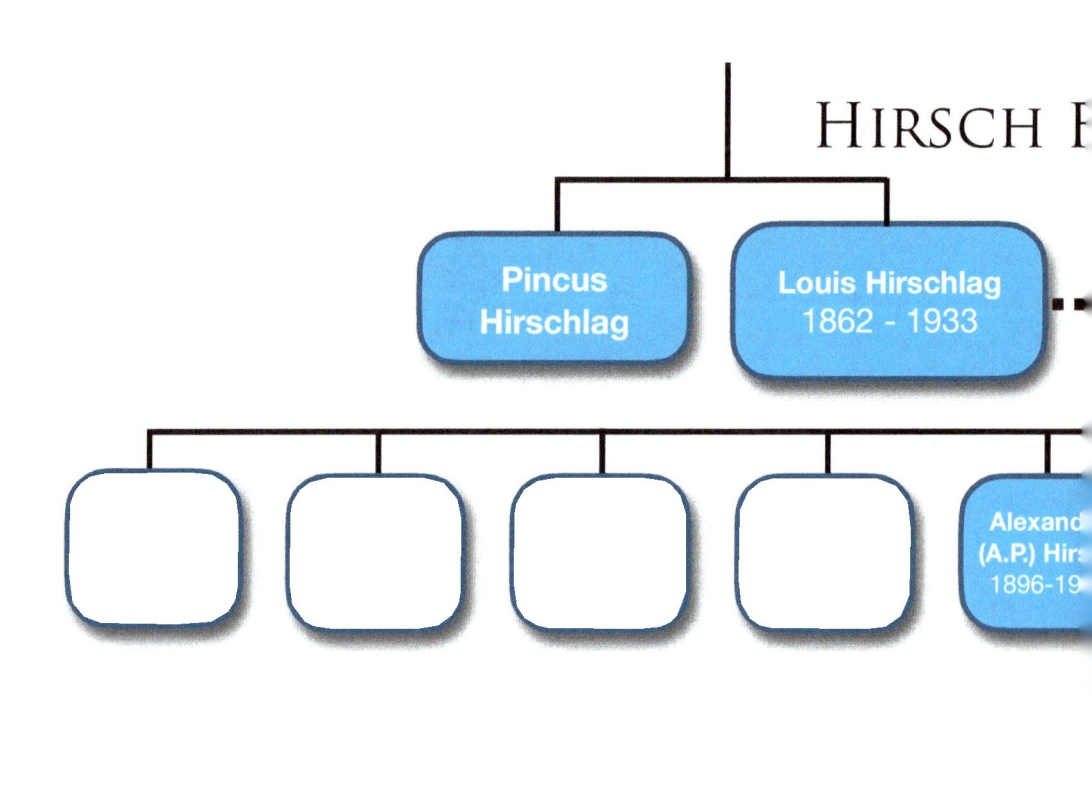

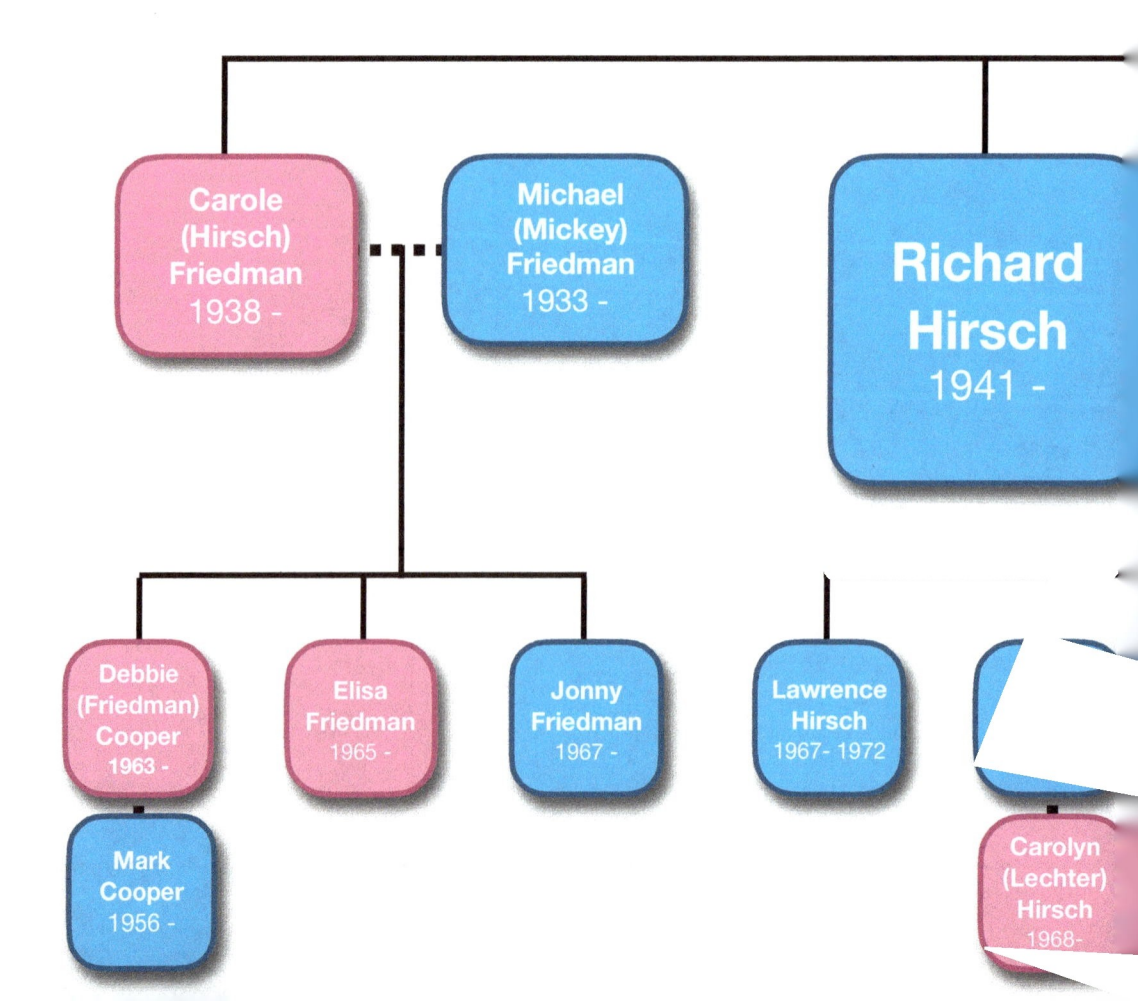

Richard L. Hirsch

HIRSCH F

- **Pincus Hirschlag**
- **Louis Hirschlag** 1862 - 1933

- **Alexand (A.P.) Hirs** 1896-19

- **Carole (Hirsch) Friedman** 1938 -
- **Michael (Mickey) Friedman** 1933 -
- **Richard Hirsch** 1941 -

- **Debbie (Friedman) Cooper** 1963 -
- **Elisa Friedman** 1965 -
- **Jonny Friedman** 1967 -
- **Lawrence Hirsch** 1967 - 1972

- **Mark Cooper** 1956 -

- **Carolyn (Lechter) Hirsch** 1968 -

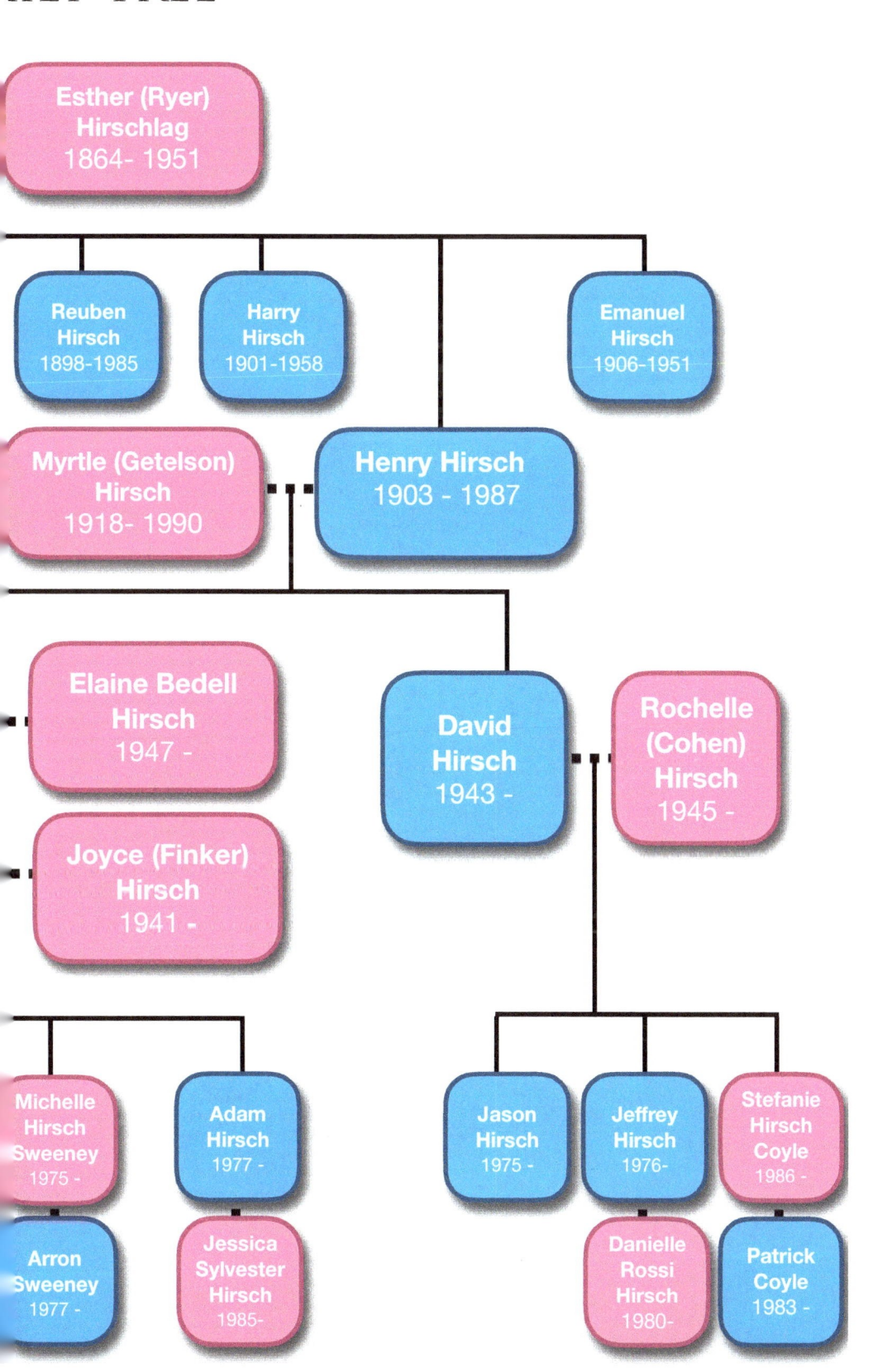

Sempre Avanti!

FAMILY TREE

Esther (Ryer) Hirschlag
1864- 1951

Reuben Hirsch
1898-1985

Harry Hirsch
1901-1958

Emanuel Hirsch
1906-1951

Myrtle (Getelson) Hirsch
1918- 1990

Henry Hirsch
1903 - 1987

Elaine Bedell Hirsch
1947 -

David Hirsch
1943 -

Rochelle (Cohen) Hirsch
1945 -

Joyce (Finker) Hirsch
1941 -

Michelle Hirsch Sweeney
1975 -

Adam Hirsch
1977 -

Jason Hirsch
1975 -

Jeffrey Hirsch
1976-

Stefanie Hirsch Coyle
1986 -

Arron Sweeney
1977 -

Jessica Sylvester Hirsch
1985-

Danielle Rossi Hirsch
1980-

Patrick Coyle
1983 -

Richard L. Hirsch

ABOUT THE AUTHOR

Richard L. Hirsch is the former C.E.O. of the Welbilt Corporation, one of the nation's largest manufacturers and distributors of commercial kitchen equipment. He is currently a principle in the Concurrent Industries Group, a New York City family investment office.

Mr. Hirsch's devotion to philanthropic endeavors has elevated him to the top leadership ranks in a number of major charitable institutions. He is the former board chairman of the Maimonides Medical Center, a non-sectarian hospital located in Borough Park, Brooklyn. Mr. Hirsch served through 2020 as the International Chairman of State of Israel Bonds.

Mr. Hirsch's "hands-on" dedication to worthy causes has earned him numerous recognition awards as well as the respect of world leaders.

He lives in Palm Beach, Florida with his wife, Elaine.

Richard L. Hirsch